Offshore Crew

By the same author

Teach Your Child About Sailing
Sails
Dinghy Sails
Night Intruder
The Care and Repair of Sails
Practical Pilotage for Yachtsmen

Jeremy Howard-Williams

Offshore Crew
Originally published as
Crewing for Offshore Racing

Illustrated by the author

ADLARD COLES LIMITED
GRANADA PUBLISHING
London Toronto Sydney New York

First published by Granada Publishing in
Adlard Coles Limited in 1973, under the title
Crewing for Offshore Racing
Reprinted 1976
Second Edition (retitled *Offshore Crew*) 1979

Granada Publishing Limited
Frogmore, St Albans, Herts AL2 2NF
and
3 Upper James Street, London W1R 4BP
Suite 405, 4th Floor, United Nations Plaza, New York, NY 10017, USA
Q164 Queen Victoria Buildings, Sydney, NSW 2000, Australia
100 Skyway Avenue, Toronto, Ontario, Canada M9W 3A6
PO Box 84165, Greenside, 2034, Johannesburg, South Africa
CML Centre, Queen and Wyndham, Auckland 1, New Zealand

ISBN 0 229 11622 1

Printed in Great Britain by
Fletcher & Son Ltd, Norwich

Contents

traveller, Cunningham hole, mast bend, mast rake, kicking strap and topping lift, hydraulics, drawstring) – Close-hauled (*light weather, medium weather, heavy weather*) – Off the Wind (*kicking strap, leechline, topping lift*) – Broaching (*preventive measures, corrective action*) *line, kedging, main anchor, tripping line, clearing a snagged anchor, fouled anchor, general anchoring tips)*

Illustrations

Photos

Drawings

Foreword

This book has the hallmark of knowledge. Jeremy Howard-Williams has been sailing for over forty years, first for fun, then as an amateur instructor in his spare time in the RAF and finally within the marine trade – so he knows his subject from the inside. His experience covers a wide range of offshore racing from 24-foot boats through 50 footers to 12 metres across-Channel and the mighty *Gitana IV*, the 90-foot ketch in which he helped establish a record for the Fastnet when he shipped as sail trimmer in 1965; he has sailed in the Baltic, Mediterranean, Indian Ocean and the Far East as well as British waters, and writes readably about all those little points which many of us take for granted, but which can so easily be overlooked by anyone starting to race seriously unless he is told about them.

This book, which any owner should lend to a new crew, ably fulfils its intention of providing a sure basis to start from. Most of what a crewman needs as a foundation finds a mention within these pages; even the rescue angle is covered from personal experience, for Jeremy spent a night in a rubber dinghy just south of the Isle of Wight in 1942 – not from a yacht it is true, but the water is just as wet jumping out of an aeroplane and it makes you just as safety conscious.

There are plenty of interesting books about sailing and plenty of informative books; I found this one both interesting and informative and am glad to have the chance of wishing it the best of luck.

Owen Parker
Southampton

Introduction

The editor originally told me that my particular brief was a book aimed at the hand who has done a bit of dinghy racing or some cruising in larger boats, and who now wants to race.

'I expect you too have had the horrible experience,' he wrote, 'of having a man recommended to you as a good hand, when what is meant is that he is good company in the bar ashore. A racing owner should be able to buy your book and, when he takes on a new crew, lend it to him and say: "Please read this right through, then I'll know what you know."'

In writing, therefore, I have assumed a certain level of seamanship in you, the crew for whom it is intended. But I have had to keep in mind that standards differ and the level of knowledge might not always be as uniformly high as the owner concerned may have been led to expect. I also found myself talking to the owner from time to time. After all, it is his responsibility to decide when to reef, how to work his watch system, whether to heave to, lie a-hull or press on in a gale and, indeed, whether to adopt a one-pole or twin-pole spinnaker gybe system. This is right and, as a new hand, you can expect to join a ship which has her basic systems all cut and dried: routine such as watches and cooking, heavy weather drill, spinnaker work and the sail wardrobe. But, even if you can't change a one-pole gybe into a two-pole system, you should know the sort of thing to expect. Not only that, you should be prepared to contribute constructive comment in discussions bearing upon the owner's sphere of influence. In the stress of offshore racing the owner has many responsibilities weighing upon his mind and he may be glad, on occasions, to be tactfully reminded of certain points (but constant prodding will drive him mad, so don't overdo it). Better still, he will certainly welcome aboard anybody who can suggest a useful job, volunteer to do it and be trusted to carry it out properly and in a seamanlike fashion.

I don't pretend to have covered everything and your own pet foible may well have been omitted. I may, indeed, hold an opposite view from your own in some cases, because part of the joy of sailing is that we don't all act the same way in a given set of circumstances. But I hope that my efforts will offer a framework onto which any owner from JOG to Class I can build, by expanding my ideas in some places and disagreeing with them in others. If he reads it before he lends it to you, his new crew, he will have a good idea of what you can do and he will understand your point of view better. Who knows, he may even pick up a few tips himself.

I would like to thank Owen Parker of *Morning Cloud* for not only reading the script but kindly writing the foreword. David Anderson of *Langston Lady*, Roger Marshall of *Quailo*, Newlyn Mason-Elliott of *Forerunner* and David Potter of *Shere Khan* were all good enough to let me have their comments on the draft typescript. I am indebted to the Editor of *Yachting World* for Appendix A, which is largely a reproduction of a table that appeared in an article by Drs G S Ingram and P J August. Dr James Arnott of *Florya* kindly read my words on seasickness in chapter 1. Messrs Lewmar Marine Limited generously supplied many of the photographs. The book would have been worse without the help of all these kind people, who should nevertheless not be held responsible for any of the opinions expressed, which are entirely my own.

Finally, I must express my deep appreciation of Bruce Fraser's help and guidance during the preparation of this volume.

1
What is a Crew?

You will hear plenty of tales of high drama offshore, told afterwards in the bar or as you assemble for the start of another race. These moments do, of course, occur, but you are more likely to remember your first offshore race as an exhausting sail with not a little monotony in it, overshadowed all the time by work which will vary according to how seriously the owner takes his racing. If he is out for a jolly, to get to France in good company, you will only work 24 hours each day; if he wants to win and reckons he has a chance, you will work a damn sight harder and for longer. Up at the sharp end offshore racing is unremitting slogging, as the skipper drives you to further effort when your aching bones scream in protest, your stomach revolts and your eyes drop from fatigue. But the fact that so many come back for more shows that there is a deep satisfaction in a job well done, a pleasure which is not entirely masochistic.

While an offshore racing crew should be properly organised, not unlike a naval crew, so that each member has clearly defined duties and, indeed, clearly defined times for doing them, it must not be inflexible. As a member of such a crew, you should understand something of everybody's job so that you can substitute if necessary. Indeed, on the smaller yachts you will find yourself doing jobs which would be covered by two or three people where more bodies are available on larger boats.

Effort
It is not enough, moreover, to say that every crewman should be able to substitute for anybody else. Every crewman on a topline offshore racer must give 120 per cent effort all the time. This is a basic principle to which there is no exception and which brooks no alternative opinion; if anyone is not prepared to subscribe to it, then he might as well stop reading now. This doesn't mean that you have to

be constantly shinning up the mast, clearing out lockers or mending sails, for there is also no place aboard for the over-eager beaver. You may, indeed, not be able to mend a sail, and nobody will think the worse of you for not possessing a particular skill. But if a sail is torn and needs to be taken down in a hurry, you should be there when required and should help prepare the sail for repairs by the man who is to wield the needle and palm. Even if you are watch below, you should be ready to rise from your bunk to help set the thing again when repairs are complete, and should stay on deck long enough to be sure that it is trimmed to the helmsman's liking, with the replacement sail not only cleared off the foredeck but stowed away properly read for use again.

This permanent giving of effort must continue until the end of the race. It sounds obvious and easy enough but, when the boat has been through a gale and you are wet and cold, when the final buoy has been turned and you are on the last leg home, when the wind is on the quarter so the kite is up and there is neither danger of broaching nor gybing, then it is that effort is liable to relax, concentration to wander. Stay with it, keep on top, and your boat will gain those precious seconds which make all the difference between saying: 'Let's fill it with champagne,' and: 'If only we'd bothered to gybe instead of running by the lee, we might have saved our time.'

If, at the very outset, I am giving a gloomy picture of hard work with no time for fun, then I offer no apology. For, make no mistake about it, racing offshore *is* hard work and the rewards will come slowly and only with time. The smaller the boat, the less possibility there is of a passenger being carried, and the greater the workload on each crew member.

This brings me to my next points: food and sleep. An engine will not work without fuel and your body is no exception. So you have to eat properly. Work also brings fatigue, so you have to sleep. Note that I don't say sleep properly, because your chances of eight hours uninterrupted slumber are nil. You will get such sleep while on watch below as you can snatch and as the heaving sea and the noises of the boat being worked will allow (always supposing that you are not called on deck to change sails or reef). Both these aspects of racing offshore are important enough to warrant expansion before we go any further. I shall refer back to them from time to time throughout the book, but only in passing, so let us examine them a little more closely now.

1 *Dolce far Niente* Wet weather in *Gitana IV* on the way out to the Rock in 1965. I am at the wheel wearing the sailing jacket I designed; note the safety line. The guitar isn't standard equipment but the three coffee grinders aft are. *Gitana* is 90 feet long, so there was plenty of room to stow the guitar! *Author*

Food

You will not be shipping as cook on your first offshore race, but you may be called upon to do your share. Some crews take it in turns to do the cooking for a day each.

For some of us, what food we eat, and when, is closely allied to the problem of seasickness; I shall come on to that later.

Victualling a yacht for an offshore race is outside the province of this book. The cook should start with a rough plan of what he intends to serve each day, which will help him buy his food and stow it where he can reach it when he wants it; don't complain

3

about the impossibility of finding the cocoa when you want it or you may, indeed, find yourself doing the cooking on your first race.

One of the requirements of cooking at sea is ease of preparation, for meals may have to be served in a hurry or in rough weather. The diet will, therefore, inevitably be based largely on tinned soups and stews, but imaginative use of curry powder, cheese, herbs and wine in the cooking can do much to relieve the monotony. It is as much a mistake to eat too much as it is to take too little. Excessive fats or rich food will make you sleepy and livery, whereas too little nourishment will weaken you. Take every opportunity to eat fresh vegetables and fruit: raw carrots, lettuce, tomatoes, apples, etc. Grapes are especially good, though hard to stow. From time to time dip into the hard tack tin which should be provided with biscuits, crisp-bread, cheese, barley sugar, dried apricots, raisins and the like.

Don't be afraid to eat bread, jam or cheese which has mould growing on the outside; if the green part is cut off, the inside is quite palatable and beggars can't be too choosy on a long race.

Liquid

An empty stomach filled with liquid will not help if you turn into your bunk, feeling a little queasy, with a cup of coffee or tea; the liquid will slop about inside you and merely add to your discomfort. And don't forget that what goes in has to come out sooner or later. It is a common practice to brew up just as you leave the moorings for the start of a race. This means that you will probably want a pee just after the race has begun; if it is blowing hard and you are short tacking among a lot of other boats, you will not only have to desert your post at a critical time, you will have to fight your way out of your oilskins just after you have fought your way into them. Basically, therefore, at the start of a race don't drink more than you have to.

Cleanliness

Many owners rightly require all meals to be taken down below. Eating in the cockpit can be messy, especially if a minor crisis disturbs the meal; it is certainly distracting for the helmsman. When you have finished, the cook will be pleased with a hand at the washing up and, if you are brewing up during the night watch, see

4

that you clean all mugs, saucepans, etc. In this connection, don't make too much noise or light when making tea or coffee in the middle of your watch; those asleep won't bless you if you allow the kettle to whistle cheerfully until the whole ship is awake.

Sleep

You should try to join ship the day before the race, so that you sleep your first night aboard in harbour. It will not only enable you to find out where everything is stowed, but you will also be able to prepare your bunk and allow your system to get used to the idea of sleeping afloat.

A bunk should, besides being as comfortable as you can make it, be as dark as possible. If it has a canvas leeboard, therefore, you

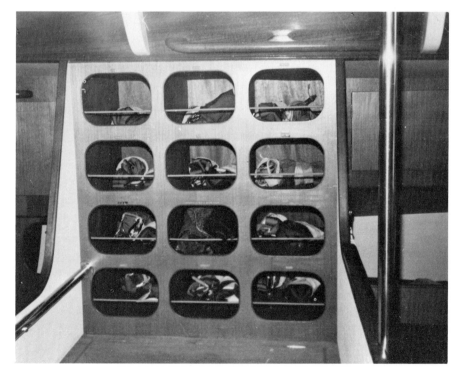

II *Personal stowage* Crew's stowage in *Quailo*. Each compartment is labelled and has shockcord across the front to hold belongings inside. *Author*

5

should rig it even if you don't think you will need it to stay in bed. Sleeping pills during the race are not recommended because they will probably leave you feeling drowsy after the usual four hours sleep, so only take them if you do, indeed, sleep aboard in harbour on the first night, thereafter put them away for the rest of the race. Anti-seasick pills may have a tranquillising side effect so, if you use them, they may double as sleeping pills.

Some sort of watch system will, of course, be adopted throughout the race, usually based on the time-honoured four hours on and four hours off principle (more of which anon). The start is a period of tension and excitement, with all hands on deck contributing to the working of the yacht in confined waters. I won't jump into a description of what is involved at this stage, but come with me to the point where the start has taken place and the fleet has settled down on the first leg of the course. It may be only seven or eight o'clock in the evening, with the sun still fairly high in the sky. But suddenly you look around on deck and you notice that one or two faces are missing. These are the old hands and they are already below in their bunks. Even if they are not asleep, they are conserving energy instead of rushing around the deck, peering through binoculars at other boats, or nipping up and down the companionway to the chart or the race card on useless missions.

Social

Despite all the warnings of work and discomfort, there is much fun in offshore racing (or we would not go on taking part). So you need to be a chap who will get along with others and who can contribute to the social life of the boat, both afloat during the race and ashore when you get to the far end. Naturally in a small community closely confined for a period of days, irritating personal habits are going to have an exaggerated effect, particularly towards the end of the race. You should therefore examine your habits and try to eliminate those which will act as a burr under the saddle. Don't clear your throat every five minutes while on watch at night, or sniff while in your bunk. Don't be an over-eager do-gooder chanting 'Jeremy Howard-Williams says that this or that is a good idea,' as you smugly put something right or make yet another maddeningly complacent suggestion. Even the regular use of certain catch phrases

6

can become infuriating after a while: 'That's the way the grapefruit squirts, my friend.'

It goes without saying that, as you would be annoyed by unnecessary talk, loud or soft, at night by the watch on deck because it would disturb your rest, so you should remember to keep conversation to the minimum in the small hours. This rule, in fact, applies not only to night time. Helming a racing yacht to get the best from her requires a degree of concentration not always appreciated by those who haven't done it, particularly under spinnaker or going to windward. Idle chatter will only distract the helmsman as well as disturb the watch below, so it can but contribute discord to the boat. Cut it out.

You will find that a well run yacht, with harmony of purpose, effort and ability, will soon build a corporate morale which will lift her crew over the bad patches. Naturally you should cherish such a spirit and do your best to foster it, so that it enables the crew to continue giving their best, not only as the race comes towards its conclusion when everybody is tired, but also as the season progresses and the temptation is to slacken the effort as people get stale. To stay at the front of the fleet requires continued determination and hard work, long after the others have given up.

Learning

If you are not a fully experienced offshore racing man, you will hope to learn more as you go on. It is better to do this from an experienced crewman rather than from the owner or skipper. This is because these two have enough on their plates concerning the campaigning, safe navigation and tactical handling of the yacht, without having to worry whether a novice has grasped the principles of stopping a headsail or bagging up a spinnaker. A fellow crew member, however, will be able to give more of his time, and he will also speak from the viewpoint of the crewman rather than the owner – often an interesting difference!

Requirements

What, therefore, will an owner look for in an aspiring crewman? He will want to know what plus points you can contribute to his team.

What is your general sailing experience? Have you been offshore? Can you be trusted alone at night on the foredeck? On the helm? Are you seasick? Will you work, work until you are ready to drop, and still be first on deck when all hands are called?

You, on the other hand, will want to know what the exercise is liable to cost you, in cash as well as effort and time. Some clubs (the RORC is one) require a fee from each boat based on the size of the crew. For most races this comes to less than the cost of a quick lunch for each man; the money goes towards administration of the race. Owners differ in their attitude to this crewing fee, which is logically the crew's responsibility. Some owners are extremely generous and pay the fee and all the victualling themselves. Others quite rightly leave the fee to the crew, but provide food and drink. Still others ask for help with the day to day living expenses of the boat; this is usually a daily sum about equal to the crewing fee. Before you decide to criticise the owner who asks you to pay both the general crewing fee and a sum towards your keep, you should remember the other high expenses sustained by an owner just to keep the boat afloat in which you are enjoying yourself: depreciation, insurance, repairs, replacements and maintenance all go on even if the boat is not racing, summer and winter, week in and week out. But you still won't pay more than you would for one or two nights in a hotel, depending on the length of the race and how much you reckon to spend while in port. On some boats it is a nice custom to dine the owner ashore at the end of the race, as an expression of gratitude for a good time. On others, a particularly memorable trip may be commemorated, in the absence of a prize, by a present from the crew to the owner; an inscribed beer mug or ashtray may require a small subscription from each man depending on the size of the crew and quality of the gift. I remember racing to Cherbourg with my stepfather T.C. Ratsey in his 50 foot sloop *Evenlode* when we were nearly all sick. We gave him a silver ashtray to remind him of his goodnatured taunts during the race; it was inscribed 'From the passengers'.

What therefore are your chances of getting a berth on an offshore race? Obviously an owner will have more difficulty in filling his crew for races which take more than a long weekend. If you can get a week off, your chances are already improved; and if you can help bring the boat back home from her port of destination, you will be more welcome still. As you might expect, the successful boats are harder to get into than those which finish consistently lower than halfway down the fleet.

Offshore racing sorts out the men from the boys. But don't be put off because you don't have a lot of experience. If you are a good dinghy man and/or have done some big boat cruising, you will know the parts of a boat, can probably be counted on to do the right thing at the right time and will know what is meant when an order is given in nautical language. You are already half way there. If you add a sense of balance, so that you can be counted on for foredeck work at night or in heavy weather, your chances must improve. An assurance that you are a glutton for hard work and are not afraid of the dirty jobs (cleaning out an oily bilge or stripping a winch) should clinch it. The owner will have reservations about you, particularly until he has seen whether you suffer from seasickness, but he will probably give you a go.

Seasickness

'There is only one certain cure for seasickness,' I was informed recently and, on my excited enquiry, was told: 'Go and sit under a tree.'

The issue is a real one offshore, for it not only affects the efficient working of the boat as far as winning the race is concerned, but it can become a positive danger in bad weather, just when a full strength crew is important. I don't want to sound alarmist, but the problem is of sufficient consequence not to be dismissed in a single paragraph. If you are one of the fortunates with an iron stomach, you may gratefully skip this section (but remember that different motions have different effects; you may be impervious to the slam of a dinghy or the chop of sheltered waters, yet the swell and send of the open sea may still turn your stomach).

Fortunately for sailing, seasickness in small boats also affects the fighting services when they are required to conduct combined operations: it is no use mounting a complicated seaborne assault supported by sea and air forces, if the troops are to be put ashore in a semiconscious condition. There have thus been some pretty high powered trials to seek a prevention or cure.

Seasickness results from upset of the balance system which is incorporated in the human ear (those who are totally deaf are usually immune from the problem). There is a delicate mechanism of tubes, liquids and sensory hairs between the inner and outer ears which, when rhythmically disturbed over a period, causes nausea and vomiting. This is aggravated if the reports of the eyes give the lie to the information received by the balance motors. In other words you see a fixed cabin with a horizon moving up and down past the window, when in fact the horizon is fixed and the cabin is moving (and your balance motor tells you so). There is disagreement as to whether diet increases a person's liability to seasickness. It seems logical to suppose, however, that an excess of fatty foods, which might lead to an upset stomach ashore, will at least be inclined to do the same at sea, if not more so; all are agreed that alcohol should be avoided. Keep fit, watch your intake of fats and acids for a week before the race and lay off the bottle, particularly if you are inclined to acidity in any case.

It is comforting to know that some medical authorities claim that modern drugs can prevent seasickness in 75 per cent of cases, if they are taken in time. If seasickness has started before remedial measures are taken, it will be difficult to keep the drug down so that it has a chance to enter the system, and recourse will have to be made to suppositories. Prevention is thus better than cure.

The requirement for offshore racing is to find a pill which will prevent or remove the nausea, without having side effects which might affect a man's efficiency (it doesn't matter if you get sleepy on a cross channel steamer, but you need your wits about you on the foredeck of a racing yacht).

Most of the proprietary seasick pills belong to the antihistamine group. There are various drugs within this category and, in general, they can be said to need several hours before they take effect, when they act for a period which varies from 8–16 hours. Some work better than others and every individual is different in the way he reacts to almost any drug he takes; this is particularly true with antihistamines. You must test your personal reactions before the drug is needed in anger. Some antihistamines are available in suppository form. See Appendix A for specific comments on individual drugs and brands; Dramamine works well in many cases because, as well as being useful for the actual sickness, it is helpful in many medical conditions which involve giddiness. The hyoscine group has shown up consistently well in military trials for short term results (three or four hours protection) and needs only be taken an hour or so before sailing. It has few side effects in the short term, but use over a period can lead to a dry mouth, blurred vision and even dizziness, particularly in the elderly. It is not readily available in suppository form. See Appendix A for brand names; Kwells are as good as any.

A drug worth special mention is Stugeron, largely because of some impressive trials organised by *Yachting Monthly* in 1978. Almost nine out of ten people reported favourably, and some had dramatic results; side effects appeared to be low.

Tranquillisers

Normal tranquillisers have little effect on seasickness, thus tending to support the view that psychological factors are of no great account in the problem. They should be avoided because of their general soporific effect.

John Illingworth has written some wise words on the question in *Further Offshore*. In common with others he advocates a careful diet for a week beforehand: avoid fats, red meats and alcohol as promoters of acidity (no grease, fried food, little butter; fish in preference to meat; and cut out those drinks). Eat plenty of salads and vegetables. Some medical opinions hold that this is a waste of time because it is perfectly normal to have acid secretions in the stomach, indeed they take part in the normal digestive process. People who tend to go on pouring out stomach acid between meals usually have digestive troubles such as ulcers, and know all about antacids anyway. But the chronic suffer from seasickness will clutch at any straw and at least pre-race dieting can do no harm.

When you come to being aboard, with seasickness more than an academic problem which can be shrugged off with good advice, you have to do something right away because a seasick crewman can be a hindrance and a danger to the whole boat. Once again we must think in terms of prevention if possible. Constipation promotes malaise and leads to seasickness, while lack of exercise and the continuous tension on a boat promote constipation. So one of the

11

obvious preventives is regular bowel movement, and this means use of the correct laxative. Don't forget it.

Having taken such precautions as are reasonable, you may still be struck down. Further preventive measures in the early stages can take the form of chewing gum or sucking barley sugar, which contains a high proportion of glucose. Looking at the stable horizon may help a little. You should get out of wet clothes if you can, because cold and damp promote seasickness. Fresh air is to be preferred to a stuffy cabin possibly filled with cooking smells or tobacco smoke but, if you do feel sick and don't recover as soon as you have vomited, lie down in a darkened bunk if you can, preferably on your side with your eyes closed.

Some people advocate eating dry biscuits as you go to your bunk, others say leave a tender stomach alone. Only you can say what suits you best – but do whatever you find helps you and don't necessarily take all the advice you will undoubtedly be given. At all events, it is now too late to take a pill because you will almost certainly bring it up again; insert a suppository the other end.

If duty is going to call in a short while and it is not possible to get into a berth, I personally prefer to stay in the fresh air on deck; others may find it more helpful to sit below with the body free to move and balance the motion of the yacht. In any case use as little energy as possible. The wise man will have provided himself with sickbags, rather like the airlines, so that he does not have to keep rushing on deck either in underwear in the cold, or else using up badly needed energy by struggling into wet weather gear each time he needs to go. Some skippers, in fact, insist that the afflicted be sick into a bucket at all times; this avoids the danger of falling overboard and also ensures that false teeth don't get lost!

The great thing when racing is not to let seasickness get the better of you, but to carry on pulling your weight. Beware, however, of your determination not to let the side down being such, that you find yourself on the foredeck in so weak a condition that you hinder everyone else and become dangerous. The problem is so universal that you will get plenty of sympathy and understanding, provided you don't use it as an excuse for dodging the column. On a long race it may be a help to know that most people's systems seem to get over seasickness after 48 hours, even though a *change* of motion may bring it on again.

To sum up: prevention is better than cure; prepare your stomach; keep the bowels moving; use the right pills; keep warm and don't waste energy; keep going.

Psychological

You are bound to be a bit apprehensive as you start racing offshore and I hope that, like me, your first one or two races will be completed in fair weather. To the tyro on his first night watch the night always looks darker, be the moon never so big, and the waves higher, be the sea never so calm. The boat appears to be rushing headlong into eternity in half a gale, with the wind whistling in the rigging and the water boiling past the hull, so steady up and take your cue from the older hands. Get up against a solid part of the boat and try to find a routine chore to do as you first come on deck. Tidy any empty cups from the cockpit, note the log reading or ask if the headsail needs trimming. By the time you have done the job, your system will be a little bit readier to accept the unusual effect of night sailing.

If indeed you are caught in a gale on one of your first night watches, it will be bad luck (it may surprise you to learn that the odds are very much against it during the average offshore race). Even more important is it that you should take your cue from the watch leader. He will not only know what to do, he will also know how to do it. This may sound banal, but tempo and precision are both involved here; a controlled energy is what is wanted, with everyone knowing what to do before the job is attempted. On some yachts a gale may not require those below to turn out, the duty watch being able to change headsails and roll down a respectable reef, but it is more than likely that you will be called on deck. Don't rush aimlessly about the place, trying to do everything at once. You will only increase the risk of being blown overboard and wasting all the time (and more) that you have been trying to save. Your thoughts should turn towards your safety equipment, and I have devoted a whole section to this later. Suffice it to say here that you should wear buoyancy and harness, as these give you a well founded sense of better security, and take great care as you first come on deck; you are at greatest risk at this time, for you may be caught unawares by a sudden gust as you come through the hatch.

13

During a gale the most obvious phenomena are the power of the wind and the size of the waves. The wind will make a lot more noise than you would have thought possible, but its principal effects will be on anything which tries to impede its free movement from A to B, and this includes the sails and your own person. The motion of the sea will cause the yacht to take on an entirely different movement as she thrusts over or through the waves, while heeling to the strength of the wind. But she has been built to withstand this treatment and you will soon find cause for satisfaction, if not enjoyment.

Under the psychological heading I must repeat the injunction to maintain concentration. After 24 hours in fine or foul weather a threshold of fatigue is reached and it is all too easy to relax one's efforts. It is now that character shows and that the personality of the owner will be put to the test as he tries to maintain enthusiasm. Your support may make all the difference to his efforts to rouse the rest of the crew for a final spurt, so keep cheerful and keep going.

2
Joining Ship

Preparation

Having succeeded in getting a berth for a particular race, there is quite a lot you can do to get ready for the big day. As I mentioned in the previous chapter, you can start preparing your stomach a week or so in advance: diet, plenty of sleep and cut down on alcohol.

Hands

You may find, particularly at the beginning of the season, that your hands are soft. Sore palms will ruin the race for you, for you will have to carry on working and you will have to avoid complaining if you don't want to drive everybody else mad. Of course, if you are a countryman you should have no trouble, but the city dwellers will have to think of some substitute for gardening or chopping down trees.

When I did the Fastnet race in Baron de Rothschild's 90 foot yawl *Gitana IV*, I had been sailing as helmsman in a Dragon all season. As the only Englishman among 18 Frenchmen, I was specially keen not to let petty ailments put me out of action, so I paid extra attention to my hands. It proved fairly easy to rig a couple of ropes under my desk and I drew my hands along them at regular intervals during the day for three or four weeks beforehand; this worked very well. Another ploy which I use at the start of each season is to walk for a mile most mornings and take with me a walking stick, round which I have put three or four seizings just to roughen it up a bit. Rubbing my hands up and down this stick hardens the palms most satisfactorily. This could be done while sitting in an armchair, but my dogs advise me that it is not nearly so effective this way; they won't let me even consider putting two or three seizings on the steering wheel of my car to achieve the same object . . .

Nails

A fistful of flogging sailcloth can be hard on the nails, even if you do use the dodge of curling your fingertips inwards as you grab the sail. Equally, long toenails can be uncomfortable stuffed into tight seaboots for lengthy periods. Make with the nail scissors, therefore, before you leave home.

The Course

You should find out something about the race you are to join, even if only to be able to talk intelligently about it aboard. What is the course? When is the start? Where are the start, the turning marks, the finish? What will the tide be doing at the start? What is the main opposition? What is your own yacht's rating? If you can locate a chart, it is worth noting the characteristics of the various turning marks (lights, shape and colours) so that you know what you are looking for; if you turn out to be the first to spot a particular buoy, you will have made a real contribution. If you know the distance between each mark, you will have a rough idea of how long you will be on each leg, and the rest of the crew won't be forever having to keep you up to date.

Familiarisation

If the owner rings you up to ask you to join him for an inshore day race round the cans a week or two before the big one, jump at it. This will provide invaluable experience of the boat under working conditions and will help you get to know the rest of the crew. All points listed below will be covered in the more relaxed atmosphere of day sailing, when the crew will not be divided into watches, so there should be plenty of hands to work the ship and still spare time for your questions.

Joining Instructions

Some owners send out joining instructions to cover many of the points a newcomer will want to know. I have put a typical example at Appendix B and a glance through it will show the sort of thing it deals with. If you do not get such instructions, you should contact the owner and raise some of the more relevant points.

You need to know whether you should bring a sleeping bag; you usually do, but some boats have a supply and it takes up too much room to have a surplus aboard. I have an inner bag made from a sheet sewn together, so that I do not dirty somebody else's bag nor do I have to rub against what may be rather a greasy surface. You will usually find that most yachts provide life jackets and safety harnesses, but you should check on this point because, apart from anything else, it is a standard safety requirement that each crew-man shall have them. I shall have more to say on this subject later, because it is so important.

Ask what limit there is on clothing, particularly if the yacht is not a Class I boat with plenty of hanging space. Special mention should be made of shore-going clothes: should you take them or not (some owners require you to send them on ahead by post)?

You could find out the reaction to an offer to contribute to the commissariat. If the ship is either 'dry' or stocked up with booze already, you should ask whether there is anything else you can bring along, such as a cold chicken or a Dutch cheese.

Gear

Apart from the camera we discuss later in this chapter, the other principal item *not* to take sailing is a suitcase. I know that the time-honoured list also includes grand pianos, umbrellas, wheelbarrows, naval officers and women, but certainly the last two have been proving this false for a long time. At all events, equip yourself with a soft duffel bag, kit bag or some form of zippered dunnage bag or holdall made of proofed cotton or synthetic cloth. This will stow in a confined space, will not knock delicate equipment and can double as a pillow at night.

Clothing

Into this bag you should put two complete changes of clothing (underwear, socks and shirts); three sweaters (one short sleeved); two pairs of slacks, at least one of which should be of heavy cloth for really cold weather; a pair of long johns or pyjama bottoms for use under your slacks at night, or else a track suit (which makes the watch below ready at all times for instant emergency service on deck regardless of weather); a pair of deck shoes (I am assuming that you will wear ankle length seaboots for the journey down to join the yacht unless the weather is very hot, as this is the easiest way of carrying them – but remember to wash the soles before you go aboard). My strong advice is not to have any truck with foot-wear which is not purpose-made for sailing. Gym shoes or sneakers may be light and comfortable enough, but their composition or crepe soles will not grip on a wet deck and this could be literally lethal. If you are doing serious sailing, you should be prepared to spend some money on the equipment which will fit you for the job.

Add to your bag some half socks to wear over your ordinary socks when using seaboots at night. Many of the major airlines offer these over-socks to their passengers to wear aboard the aircraft instead of shoes; they take up little room but add greatly to the warmth of your feet. A woollen hat, or perhaps a beret, is a useful and easily stowed item of headgear which can cause no offence; a yachting cap or long-peaked baseball type hat pre-supposes a certain level of competence in the wearer (or else a naïvety proper to a complete tyro), so I should reserve these for later in the season when you have proved your usefulness as a crew member.

Oilskins

Don't forget your wet weather gear. Smocks and trousers are no longer proofed with linseed oil, but they are still referred to as oilskins. There are several principles to be considered in selection of these important garments and these include:

1 Waterproof qualities.
2 Safety (buoyancy, harness, colour).
3 Comfort (fastenings, ability to move about, warmth).
4 Durability.

Waterproof Qualities

The principal object of oilskins is to keep you dry. In bad weather, water has a way of penetrating the most secure clothing, so you can never over-insure in this respect; but you should beware of sacrific-ing mobility or comfort to this end. I always prefer trousers which are held high under the armpits by means of straps over the shoul-ders, rather than those with elastic waistbands; the latter tend to come down and leave too much chest and tummy exposed to any-thing which creeps through the jacket. There should preferably be some means of holding the legs tight round your ankles, although my personal preference is to wear my oilskin trousers outside my seaboots, so that water does not run off them and into my boots; I realise that I get a wet leg when I have to wade knee deep in water, but there is little difference between a wet leg and a wet foot, which you get more often the other way. Beware of the one-piece suit which, while being waterproof and warm, is hard to get in and out of in a hurry.

The Oilskin Top

This poses more problems than the trousers. A smock is more waterproof than a front opening jacket which goes on like a coat, but the latter is easier to put on and can be worn half open in warm weather. The smock type also tends to get you very hot under certain conditions, because condensation builds up inside so, apart from other considerations, I prefer the front opening type. This should fasten right up under the chin with a double flap and an extra neck fastening, and it should have a hood which stows away in the back of the collar; the cuffs should be able to be closed tight round the wrists.

Safety

You must consider carefully whether you want buoyancy built into your oilskin, and also whether you want an integral harness. I must say here and now that I am a firm believer in both. Before you throw up your hands in horror and start protesting about bulk and sweat, let me tell you that it *can* be done. I admit that such jackets are hard to find, so much so that I had to develop my own product some years ago.

Buoyancy

I started with the principle that I wanted an oilskin jacket which you put on like a jacket; that is to say: front opening. It therefore had a nylon zipper all the way up to the neck. I realised that permanent buoyancy would make the thing unduly bulky and awkward, so I incorporated an air lung with an inner lining to the jacket for protection; this lung goes right behind the neck where it also fills the collar when inflated, thus supporting the head. On the other hand there are cogent arguments against relying solely on

19

air inflation for buoyancy, and I am the first to agree their validity; I just happen to think that its lack of bulk more than makes up for its drawbacks. A serviceable buoyancy aid, which you wear all the time and which allows you to move about freely, will be of more use than a fully approved lifejacket which either stays in a locker below or else restricts your movements to the point of being awkward and dangerous. But make sure the lung is regularly checked.

Harness

My next requirement was a harness. I am a great advocate that an 80 per cent efficient harness on your back is better than a 100 per center down in your bunk. My jacket had a nylon webbing strap high on the chest which went right round the back between the two linings (and under the lung). This strap emerged in front with a D ring at each end, one each side of the zipper opening, so that they were side by side when the jacket was zipped up. It was not adjustable in any way, but it took less than 10 seconds to put on, at night time as well as in daylight, and I was then fully buoyant and harnessed. I marketed it for a year or two but, when I left the Isle of Wight where it was made for me, I lost interest and direct contact. It is still produced by the manufacturers in very similar form and was announced in 1970 as the first sailing jacket to be granted full Department of Trade and Industry approval as a lifejacket rather than a buoyancy aid. Many is the crewman who has been turned out in the middle of the night to help reef in a gale, who has struggled with the tangle of his harness (if he can find it), only to throw it down in despair as the watch on deck encourages his early appearance to help; he then stumbles on deck half asleep with ill-adapted night vision, right where it is all happening. This is just the time when a harness is needed most, and I repeat that I would rather have a non-adjustable one round my chest than a snug fitting 100 per cent efficient one lying in a tangle down below.

Colour

Oilskins should be yellow or orange. Dark blue with a red lining is undoubtedly smart, so is white; but they serve no other purpose. A sharp contrast with the sea and spray is needed for easy spotting in case you should fall overboard. I would rather be unfashionable and alive than a smart corpse.

Comfort

As I said just now, it is important to be able to move freely in the oil-skins of your choice, and to be able to wear them in warm weather without getting into a muck sweat. Take great care in choosing them: try them on, see what kind of fastening the jacket and trousers have (complicated patent fasteners have a way of failing against the elements, so don't be lured away from buttons, zippers and grip closures), check on how difficult it is going to be to have a pee as against the likelihood of rain or spray getting inside through openings which are too easy; see that you have some sort of storm collar or hood.

Durability

Jackets with permanent buoyancy tend to be bulky, so do those which are over-thick in a laudable attempt at durable waterproof qualities. On the other hand there are oilies which are so light and thin that, even if they keep out the water to start with, they will tear easily and thus become useless, so are best left to bicyclists and picknickers. You have to strike a balance between keeping out the water, comfort (bulk and/or a tendency to make you sweat freely due to lack of aeration) and durability.

Neckwear

You must have something to put round your neck in wet weather because, with the best will in the world, no oilskin will keep out all the water which the elements can throw at you. A towel makes the ideal material, but they are usually too wide to make a reasonable scarf (or else it would be bulky and uncomfortable under the chin). You therefore either have to rip the towel in half, whereupon it proceeds to fray, or else you have to find a narrower one. The average kitchen roller towel is exactly the right width and length for the job if you cut it across the narrow width into two (and you will need two, because they get wetter than almost anything else).

Toilet Articles

I have owned an electric razor since I started shaving in 1938, so it would take a lot to persuade me to scrape my chin with a blunt instrument as Julius Caesar used to do. I have tried cordless, chargeable, pump action and battery operated razors afloat (I still have my first razor, which I used to take sailing with a hefty 110 volt dry battery) and I have now settled to one which holds its own charge for nearly three weeks. I find it a great deal easier than soap and water and a cut chin. You will also need the usual comb, soap, nail brush, tooth brush and towel; there is no need to resort to the extremes of space economy professed by a shipmate of mine as he exhibited an evil looking brush while we were stowing gear before a race:

'Clothes one end, shoes the other, hair and teeth in the middle,' he grunted proudly.

Personal First Aid

As I mentioned in the previous chapter, take your own brand of seasick pills if you have one (the purists would suggest that it would be better to take *anti*-seasick pills, I suppose); if you don't have a pet nostrum for this ailment, pick one from the list at Appendix A. Include a supply of laxatives so that your system doesn't get bunged up (and it will, believe me), together with some anti-diarrhoea preparation in case you overdo the laxatives. This evokes a ghastly picture of alternate pills being rammed into a protesting gut in a kind of hideous anal stop-go, but you might be glad of it. Barley sugar provides energy through glucose, which also helps to keep down acidity of the stomach, so take some to suck during the night watches, some people find that dry bread helps to steady the stomach. Have some lip salve or other cream to ward off sun- and wind-burn, and a pair of sunglasses to rest your eyes from the glare, particularly when you are tired and covered with salt.

Tools

You will need a good knife, either of the sheath variety or which can be opened easily with cold hands, a shackler or pair of pliers, and a marlin spike. If you are going to do a good deal of big boat sailing it is worth investing in a set of tools which can be bought in one sheath: a knife, a pair of stainless steel pliers and a marlin spike. At all events, see that your equipment is either attached to you by a lanyard or else has a cord loop on it so that you can slip it over your wrist; this will mean that you will be able to use it a second time. Add a small plastic torch (not metal because it will affect the compass more) which you won't mind losing or seeing broken, and keep it in your oilskin pocket.

General

All authorities I have read are unanimous that you should *not* take a camera, a transistor radio or your favourite musical instrument on your first race. There is no doubt that the last two can be of interest and use at varying times, but leave it to the regular crew to provide them. (Uffa Fox once designed a boat where the saloon table revealed a miniature piano when it was turned upside down.) A camera only gives rise to irritation if you are not well known to the crew. Whenever any work is to be done, the photographer is to be found playing about with his equipment instead of lending a hand, the camera has to be stowed carefully and doesn't like winch handles being dropped on it, other crew members have to make allowances and take special precautions; leave it ashore until you know them better.

Wrap your clothes in polythene bags closed by twist wires or elastic bands, if you really want to keep them dry at all times. Don't forget to stow the empty bags away carefully as you undo them because, if you throw them overboard, they will not rot in the sea but may eventually clog an engine intake if left to float free. Throw in a pair of bathing trunks and you are just about ready to go.

Joining

Some owners like their crews to be aboard 24 hours before the start of an important race. While this may be difficult to manage in our hard-pressed society, it fits in well with my recommendation in the previous chapter to do just that. It allows you plenty of time to get to know the rest of the crew and to find your way about the boat as suggested below. Equally, you will have a chance to accustom yourself to sleeping afloat for one undisturbed night, assisted or not by the only sleeping tablet you should allow yourself on the whole trip.

Punctuality

Be punctual. If you are asked to be aboard by a certain time, it may be because the owner wants to put to sea for an hour or so to try out a new sail, to catch a tide to the start or shake down the crew.

There is no surer way of creating a bad first impression than to arrive late, with the rest of the crew only waiting for your appearance to hoist sail. Don't wear hard shoes, or even deckshoes which are covered in grit from the car park.

You should spend time, as soon as you arrive, stowing your gear securely and tidily in the space allocated to you before finding out where everything is on board. Securely and tidily, I said. You will be thrown about a bit more offshore than you may be used to, and your gear will come adrift unless you think about what it is going to do on *both* tacks; so see that it is tucked well away. A small boat can quickly become a shambles unless everyone makes a real effort to be tidy at all times. An offshore racing crew usually errs on the large side compared with a cruising complement, because the boat must be workable with half the crew on watch below; you may find that you work the 'hot bunk' principle, where the man you relieve on deck climbs into your bunk as you get out of it. Such a crowd in close quarters simply *has* to be tidy, for one untidy member will not only cause chaos, but he will also rub the rest of the crew up the wrong way as they fall over his gear.

As soon as you have stowed your gear, set about finding out where everything is. You don't have to ask about every mortal thing, for a swift trip from end to end of the boat will soon reveal most. If you are all assembling only a few hours before the start, the regular crew will be busy about their routine tasks and they will not take kindly to constant interruptions from a stranger who is over-concerned about being useful. There is a happy mean to be found between the idle spectator who has to be shoved out of the way, and the eager beaver who rushes about under everyone's feet doing jobs the wrong way.

Of course you will want to help and you should ask for jobs. Don't, whatever you do, do anything without asking first, however obvious it may seem, for you may find that you will undo something done by somebody else, or you will do it wrong: if you zero the trip on the log the navigator may want the sub-total for some calculation; if you refill the cooker it may not be alcohol fuel in that labelled bottle after all, or the cook may be in the middle of a fuel consumption test.

Keep your eyes and ears open and volunteer for anything you hear about to be started and which you know you can do. Clean out

24

the tool locker, take the emergency water containers ashore for refilling, scrub the heads; the dirtier the job the better, for you want to be asked again, don't you?

Now is the time to find out where important items are kept and how they are used. It is pretty obvious that you will want to know the whereabouts of the reefing handle, the binoculars, the various instruments and the sails. What is not so easy to remember (especially on a sunny afternoon) is that it is important to know where the various light switches are located, so that you do not wake the watch below by flooding the saloon with light instead of illuminating the compass. You also need to know the whereabouts of the various seacocks and which is open and which is shut; the positions of the bilge pump and fire extinguishers; how to work the heads (if you haven't already found out by cleaning them); how to set the barometer, read the echo sounder, turn on the radio, switch the sailing instruments from 'calm' to 'rough', and locate and withdraw the electronic log impellers to clean off weed without flooding the boat. It is annoying for a watch leader to ask a hand to slip below and switch the log from automatic impeller selection to port or starboard as the case may be, only to have a blank look returned.

As soon as the general bustle dies down (or before it starts if you are all aboard early) find out if you are to have any particular responsibility. There are boats on which an attempt is made to allocate specific jobs to each man. This is all very well, providing everybody else doesn't shelve that task in the secure knowledge that it is so-and-so's job. So-and-so is watch below, or hasn't managed to come this trip, and nobody else knows how to do it. I cannot stress too strongly the importance of everybody knowing how to do everybody else's job, particularly in a small boat where the crew is limited in numbers.

You must also learn where the emergency equipment is located and how to work flares and the liferaft (the pre-race scrutineer will ask some searching questions when he comes aboard before the start, and is liable to pick on any member of the crew at random).

Watches

You will be told before the start of the race which watch system you are operating. Most are based on the well tried naval four-on four-

25

off cycle, with dog watches for changing the rhythm. But there may be local reasons for altering this method, either because the boat is overcrewed or shorthanded, or else because the owner has adopted what he considers a better system; see chapter 8 for details of various watches.

There is a great deal to be said for the owner standing out from a watch. In this way he will be available on deck when most of the tricky decisions are expected, and can be called ruthlessly from his bunk at any time in the certain knowledge that he can go below again, even if there is a change of watch. He must, of course, discipline himself to snatch sleep whenever the opportunity presents itself.

The same can be said of the navigator. If he stands a watch like anybody else, he may find that he then has to turn out during his watch below in order to plot a position or issue a new course; yet he still has to stand his watch when the time comes. If this system is adopted, it is virtually essential to have a hand in the other watch who can fill in as navigator for the simpler tasks such as taking fixes, identifying lights and plotting a position. Sometimes the owner is also the navigator, which is useful; conversely it can happen that in a crew of six, three are needed to stand watch (although more often there will be two watches of two, leaving the owner and navigator free as suggested above; they also help with reefing and sail changes, which can then be effected without calling the watch below).

During very cold or storm conditions it may be wise to reduce watches to two hours each, and certainly helmsmen should be relieved more frequently while the strain is on. Return to normal as soon as conditions permit or else, far from relieving the strain through short tricks on deck, it will increase it through repeatedly disturbed short periods of sleep.

There are those who advocate two long night watches of five or six hours each; this gives the watch below longer in their bunks. But no crew can maintain peak concentration for six hours, particularly at night, and there is a danger of wrong decisions or slack steering and sail trimming with this system.

From a crew's point of view, watches arranged so that they can be fairly sure of not being disturbed when below are a good thing. It is tiring and irritating to be constantly called on deck to help hand a sail or undertake some operation which the duty watch cannot manage alone. This is why the system of two watches of two in a six man crew is a good one, for you effectively have a potential of four at all times for sail changes, reefs or gybes, by calling on the skipper and navigator when needed.

Whatever system is adopted, always remember that voices carry loudly at night from deck to bunk. Even if you don't disturb the helmsman, you will wake the watch below if you natter constantly to your fellows. Equally, someone who is for ever coming below to forage for biscuits, even if he only uses a torch, will disturb those sleeping as he ferrets among tins and packages with clash and rustle. You will shortly be the one trying to sleep, so do unto others . . . When the time comes to change watches, always brew up just before you rouse those who are to relieve you, so that they wake to a hot cup of tea or coffee if they want one. The very act of boiling the water will probably wake them to their duties, and before it is ready they will be stumbling from their bunks.

If you are one of those doing the stumbling make sure that you are dressed and on deck, ready to take over, in proper time. A late changeover is a sign of a slack crew and only serves to promote ill feeling.

Safety

Safety is important and you should make yourself familiar with the more routine precautions. I shall go more fully into the whole subject later on, but will overlap slightly at this point. The matter is so important that it will bear a little repeating and, in any case, it is worth summarising the various drills here so that you know what to expect and what your personal part is likely to be.

Buoyancy and Harness

The ship's rules regarding wearing buoyancy and harness must be obeyed at all times. The criteria for these will vary from boat to boat, but you will usually be required to wear a harness on the foredeck above force 4 in day time and at any time when not below at night; the limit may be lowered when carrying a spinnaker as this sail hinders turning round to pick someone up. Buoyancy may be subject to the same or slightly less stringent rules. There is, of course, nothing to stop you wearing either or both whenever you wish; some boats, indeed, require harnesses to be worn on deck whenever a man cannot swim faster than the yacht is travelling.

Man Overboard

The first and most important action when a man falls overboard is to shout a warning at the top of your voice, so that the entire crew comes on deck regardless of their state or condition. One hand should be told to keep his eye on the poor unfortunate in the drink (it is easier than you may think to lose sight of a man in the water – all you can often see is a head bobbing about between waves and, if these are big, even this disappears quickly unless kept permanently in view). One hand will throw a lifebuoy overboard as soon as the accident occurs, as this will give the lookout something more to see in the water (most offshore races have specific rules about lifebuoys, requiring whistle, dye marker, flag, self-igniting light and drogue; these all help in the task of spotting and recovery). A knowledgeable helmsman, who can be relied upon to do the right thing at the right time, will be put on the helm. If you ever hear the cry 'Man overboard!' when sailing, throw something, anything which floats, over the side instantly, then look to the skipper for orders. If none are immediately forthcoming, keep your eye on the swimmer and make a path with further floating objects (not forgetting the regulation lifebuoy); make a note of the compass course so that you can sail back along your track, and the exact time of the accident so that you know how long to sail on the reciprocal course when you have turned round. See chapter 10 for fuller details, including what to do if you go overboard yourself.

Fire

In case there is a fire aboard, you should know the location of the nearest extinguisher. Even then you should be able to recognise whether the fire is electrical, fuel, cooking fat or solid matter, and only use the correct extinguisher (water spreads a fuel or fat fire; foam will blanket most things; chemicals may be toxic in a confined space).

Shipwreck

The various stages of emergency should be known, from 'All hands on deck' to 'Abandon ship'. Where are the flares? How do they work? When should they be used (when searching craft or aircraft are heading towards you for preference, and don't go and use half a dozen at a time). Is there any emergency food; if so, where is it? Does the ship have an SOS transmitter? What are the other accepted distress signals? (Flapping the arms up and down, red flares or stars, orange smoke, continuous sounding of a fog horn, a gun or explosion at about one minute intervals, a square flag above or below a ball or sphere, code flags NC, flames or smoke on the yacht and, though not internationally recognised as such, the ensign hoisted upside down.) How does the liferaft jettison? What is the single most important item to go aboard the liferaft? (the crew).

Danger Points

There are several possible sources of emergency aboard the average racing yacht, and each should be the subject of strict discipline. Engine fuel (other than diesel) must be properly turned off when the engine is not in use, both at the tank and the engine if two cocks exist; spare cans of fuel should be properly lashed down and their caps checked regularly for leaks. Cooking fuel, be it gas, alcohol or kerosene, should be similarly treated (butane gas is well known as being heavier than air, so it will sink to the bilges and await careless ignition with eager anticipation). Emergency flares are explosive and they should not only be protected from water seepage, but also against fire risk. Seacocks have a job to do and you should know where they all are, and whether they are to be kept closed unless needed or left permanently open (if the boat is inexplicably making water, you may be told off suddenly to go and check all seacocks; it's no good forgetting the galley sink if that is where the pipe has come adrift). The stern gland is a possible source of leak, and you should know how to get at it and how to work the greaser.

Calling the Owner on Deck

The frequency with which the owner (or skipper for that matter) requires to be called on deck will vary slightly according to whether he stands a watch or not. If he also doubles as navigator, then he should definitely not form part of a watch. In any case, you should find out if he has any set rules about when he requires to be on deck. He should be available at all times and will probably spend more time up top than anyone else; when in doubt, call him up. For his part, he should not overdo things, but be content to hand over tactical command to his watch leaders and grab what rest he can when he can. If he doesn't pace himself, he will get overtired and irritable, this will spread through the crew and he will also be prone to bad decision making. He should be asked to come and have a look in the following circumstances:

1 When the safety of the boat is in doubt: a big ship heading for you is less than two miles away; an unidentified buoy has been sighted; unknown land is sighted; fog descends.

2 Wind increases so that it is necessary to reef, or the wind falls so light that speed is seriously reduced and navigational plans must be reconsidered.

3 If race strategy is in question. I make a difference here between the *strategy* of deciding whether to tack in the expectation of a windshift later (i.e. the overall plan of campaign) and the *tactics* of working the boat to best advantage along the course already decided (i.e. the hour-to-hour manoeuvring within the strategic plan).

4 A landfall, unless completely on schedule.

5 Any emergency.

3
At the Start

On the day of the start, the owner may arrive on board fairly late. All hands will have turned to, in order to get the boat as ready as possible so that she can move out as soon as he is aboard. In these circumstances he will not have time for more than a cursory chat to you as he hurries below to change and stow his gear. Now is not the time to pass on messages from mutual friends.

On the other hand, there may be anything from four to five hours before the start. In any event, this is a vital period for the new crewman who has not managed to get away for a day race or a weekend cruise in the boat before. This period will be all too short, no matter how many hours it is, for it represents just about the only time when the boat is sailing yet the pressure is not on. So make the most of it and learn your way about the deck. I have listed at Appendix C most of the points which the skipper will want to cover before the start, so have a look at it to find out what everyone else will be doing.

You will soon see who the owner turns to most often for advice and discussion, and this will be your cue to accept that man as second in command, even if he is not pointed out to you as such.

Moorings

First and foremost be on hand as the mooring warps are slipped, so that you can note which actual ropes are used, on which cleats, and where they are stowed. There are subtle differences to tying up, depending on whether you are berthed at a marina, tidal quayside, mooring piles or a swinging mooring. You will not be called upon to supervise the arrangement of warps and fenders, but it will pay to understand the basic factors involved so that you can immediately become a useful member of the team.

Marina

At a marina a boat will have little room for manoeuvre and will almost certainly move out under power. She will be berthed along-side a floating pontoon, which will rise and fall with the tide and so will maintain a constant height in relation to the yacht, regardless of the time of day. There will not be room, without crossing and fouling other yachts' warps, for head and stern ropes which stretch away fore and aft. You will be restricted to breast ropes from the bow and stern, with springs to prevent fore and aft movement.

Tidal Quayside

At a tidal quayside, the boat will rise and fall during the day so, if constant attention to mooring warps is to be avoided, precautions have to be taken. First, breast ropes will be left off, as they are too short to allow any latitude; head and stern lines, with springs as for a marina, are more in order, as they are long enough to offer some slack and stretch as the boat rises and falls on the tide. Where the tidal range is large, say over ten feet, you may find that there are mooring rings which slide up and down posts to allow for the changing height of water, but you are more likely to have to adopt some sort of system to allow movement of the boat; head and stern lines will not cope with such a large change. In this case, a sliding breast rope can be rigged along the lines of figure 2.

Mooring Piles

If you are tied up at your own mooring piles (posts), almost cer-tainly there will be some system of wire strops fore and aft, which are cut to the correct length to fit snugly over your bow and stern mooring cleats. These wires will be made fast to rings which are free to slide up and down the mooring piles and so allow for rise and fall of the tide. The two inboard ends, which fit to the boat's cleats, will be joined together by a soft line which will be buoyed; this is so that they can be picked up as a unit when the boat comes in to moor up. Frequently there are two boats to one pair of piles. If you are first boat to arrive on the moorings, it is usual to complete your own mooring arrangements and then to hoist your companion's buoy into your rigging so that it is all ready for him when he comes alongside.

If you do not have permanent strops to the piles, you will have to use your own mooring lines. These will be taken by dinghy to the pile in question and made fast to the sliding ring by a round turn and a bowline. Should you be alongside another boat, you will also be made fast to her by breast ropes and springs (the latter designed to prevent surging fore and aft, with possible danger of clashing spreaders – so see that your masts are well separated before you leave the boat). On strange piles, there is a temptation sometimes

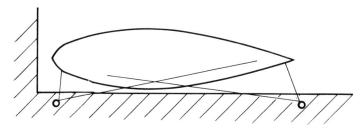

1 *Mooring at a floating berth* Breast ropes keep the boat alongside the pontoon, while fore and aft springs prevent her moving forward or astern. The springs can be a continuation of the breast ropes taken back aboard from the pontoon ring or bollard, as shown here. They may equally be formed by making one end fast to the pontoon, leading back aboard as a breast rope and then forward or aft to a ring or bollard on the pontoon about halfway along the boat.

simply to make fast to a neighbouring boat without putting out lines to the piles, especially when this involves using a dinghy, as it normally does. This is all right if you are a small boat and your neighbour is large and not about to put to sea, but even then only if the weather is calm, you are not staying long and somebody will be aboard all the time. It is unfair on your neighbour's mooring tackle to expect it to support the weight of two boats (which can some-times be increased again if another visitor comes and ties direct to you in the same manner). Always put a line fore and aft to the piles themselves as well as tying to the other yacht if there is going to be any weight on your tackle.

Swinging Mooring

Swinging moorings are becoming things of the past in many an-chorages, as they take up so much room. But they still exist in some parts of the country and they offer the somewhat selfish pleasure of a space of your own. They are easy to pick up and cast off, and you do not have to worry about a multitude of mooring warps and fenders. A point to remember is that the line which usually secures the buoy to the chain will have to be brought aboard until the chain itself arrives to be secured; this leaves a goodly length of rope on board. If you are required to cast off, beware of hurling the whole assembly willy nilly over the side with a professional cry of 'All gone for'ad!' It will take an appreciable time for the chain to sink and pull the rope down after it, some of which may be left near the surface long enough to get wrapped round the propeller as you motor away. Ease the chain over the side and allow the line to run out as you hold onto the buoy; you should then walk aft as the boat moves ahead, holding the buoy and keeping the slack clear of the side of the boat until you can thrown it all well away from the stern.

Fenders

After you have cleared moorings, all fenders should be brought inboard and stowed, for nothing looks more lubberly than a yacht sailing along, possibly feeling rather pleased with herself, but with a fender or two still hanging over the side. Note how and where the fenders are hung, although you will almost certainly not remember where they should go when you moor up again. Fender ropes should not be made fast to the guard rail or led over the top of the guard rail; they should be led under the rail and secured to a grab rail or cleat. In this way they are more secure, will maintain a constant height and won't be subject to chafe by the rail.

Making Sail

Next in chronological order as you move off comes the business of hoisting sail. You are more likely to have to lower and hoist headsails rather than the mainsail during the race, so you should try and attend to that sail as it goes up if you cannot be present at both ceremonies. Note the tack fastening (some yachts have fairly patent systems) and check that it is standard for all sails. Check the halyards at the mast until you know them by heart, and then check them again; you don't want to be the one to lower the spinnaker instead of the genoa, or the mainsail instead of the topping lift. Note how the halyard is secured and how the spare rope is stowed; if you are left to do it yourself, ask how the owner likes it done (some

34

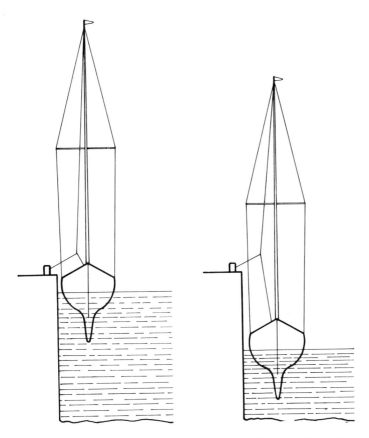

2 *Mooring at a tidal quayside* A sliding breast rope can be rigged on the main halyard (or on the cap shroud), so that it adjusts to the different height of the boat as she rises and falls on the tide. Make sure that the ring or shackle is free running. Springs and head and stern lines, being longer, can be rigged to allow some latitude of movement, but they will need tending if the rise and fall is great.

owners won't have any rope whatever made fast to a cleat with a half hitch, preferring to leave the lazy end entirely free of encumbrance).

When all sail is set, check the functioning of ancillary sail controls so that you don't have to ask again (we will examine their correct use later):

1 Mainsail clew outhaul, leechline, Cunningham, tack down-haul, reefing system, sheet traveller, kicking strap.
2 Headsail halyard, downhaul if fitted, Cunningham hole, leech-line, fairlead adjustment, Barber hauler.

35

Have another look at the spinnaker pole or poles. Get the boss of the foredeck to show you how it is rigged, preferably by physically taking it from its stowage and clipping it onto the mast with its topping lift and downhaul rove. Note where the topping lift and foreguy are cleated, so that you can put your hand on them without further question by night and by day. Check the spinnaker sheet and guy system, and see where they are rove and cleated.

If the boat has a numbering system for halyards and fairleads, so that particular sails can be trimmed in particular winds to predetermined settings, find out where the master check list is kept so that you can locate it again in a hurry. Have a look at winch operation and handle stowage, see how the helmsman likes the mainsheet made up and learn to work the mainsheet traveller adjustment.

Often a crew member who does not normally steer will take the helm on leaving harbour. This allows the starting helmsman time to have a last minute check of the starting line, a quick conference with the navigator and the owner, and to get himself ready for the race. You should take your cue from the others and make your own personal preparations in plenty of time.

A quick look at the sail locker will probably reveal a marked difference from the evening before. The mainsail and genoa will have gone, for one thing, and probably one of the spinnakers as well. The rest of the sailbags will have been arranged so that they can be identified and extracted easily. So you should set about checking on their basic differences forthwith, unlearning all you thought you had safely assimilated earlier.

When you have got all you usefully can from the pre-start period, get yourself ready at least half an hour before the gun. This involves three points:

1 Bladder
2 Dress
3 Job

First, have a pee. You may be required for continuous deck duty after the start, or you may be dressed in oilies, which do not exactly make a trip to the heads the quick slash of the pub crawler. Secondly, get into the correct rig for the first couple of hours. More often than not this will turn out to be sweaters and oilskins, and you don't want to be the only one in your watch to take time off below after the start to

36

dress up properly. On the other hand, don't overdo it but take your cue from the others if in doubt. Finally, make sure that you know what your job at and just after the start is to be, and then go and do it.

The Start

Keep your eyes open at all times. The nursery period is now over and you are one of the team, so you share equally with the rest of the crew a corporate responsibility for correct handling of the boat. If you see something obviously awry, tell the watch leader and then fix it. If you haven't got a specific job, don't go and hang about in the most convenient place for spectating – this will almost certainly be slap in the middle of the main hatch, halfway down the companionway and, while out of the way of the winch men, the boom, the helmsman and the instruments, it blocks the passage of the navigator as he dashes below to make a frantic last minute check on the inner distance mark, or of the owner as he dives in disbelief for the tidetable, or of the watch leader searching vainly for a handy-billy. Get up on the weather deck and lie still and, above all else, quiet. During the count-down period only the voices of the navigator telling the time and the helmsman informing the crew of his intentions should be heard. At this time the helmsman's brain will be humming like a computer as he assesses course, speed, distance, time, tidal stream and other boats. He may be forgiven if his nerve ends show (they should not, but most helmsmen are human) and if he snaps a little when he doesn't get an immediate answer to such queries as:

'How many minutes?'

'What have I got?'

'All clear to leeward?'

If you have sailed a bit before, possibly in dinghies, there may be a temptation to assess the quality of the start and to voice your thoughts. Don't. You can but be a distraction with an unqualified opinion, possibly based on false information (wrong starting line or incorrect timing) and certainly on an inexperienced assessment of the boat's speed and capabilities and on ignorance of the helmsman's intentions. As I said just now, however, you share responsibility for the proper navigation of the yacht and must be prepared to contribute your two penn'orth if you see danger threatening (in the form of a right of way yacht under your lee, a buoy in the way or a large baulk of timber floating in the water on your course). But leave the tactics to somebody else.

If you are asked to go forward and keep a check on whether the boat is over the line, and you are either unsure of the line or are not used to judging whether you are going to be over a transit (or, more difficult, over a line joining a committee boat at one end to a marker buoy at the other, where there is no transit but you have to look both ways to see whether you are over the line), then say so instantly. If things are close, much may depend on your assessment of the yacht's position and you must be sure that you know what you are doing.

Until the owner gets to know you a bit better, on your first race you will probably not be allocated anything more glamorous just before the start than pulpit watch when jockeying for the line. This is an important job, particularly when you are in close company with other yachts, and you should give it your complete attention. It is all very exciting to see the big names in offshore racing as they tack or bear away around you but don't get too involved, because your helmsman is relying on you to spot that starboard tack yacht hidden from him by his genoa, in plenty of time for easy evasion and not after she has become a crisis. If you have done a good deal of hot dinghy racing, you may well find yourself the most knowledgeable man aboard as far as the racing rules are concerned, so sit up and take notice.

The pulpit may be a wet job, so this is another reason for putting on oilies before the start – only those already wearing the right clothes can be considered for the task and you don't want to produce shortcomings in your first ten minutes of offshore racing. The position to adopt is a sitting one right forward, either with your back to the pulpit and one leg each side of the forestay, facing aft, or else lying on your side to windward of the forestay, looking round it to leeward. You can then see through the arc which is blind to the helmsman, you can hold on, and you disturb the airflow over the genoa as little as possible. When the boat tacks you will be able to gather the genoa along the foot to draw it forward a bit and thus help it round the mast.

Routine

As soon as the fleet has settled down and spread out after the start and you have been called aft from your pulpit duties, sort out your routine. If you are watch below, then get below straight away. It is all very exciting checking up on your rivals and watching their technique as they manoeuvre, but you will be using up reserves which you will want later. Every time you dash below for the list of competitors or the binoculars you are burning energy; lack of energy leads to lassitude and, later, seasickness. If you look around you an hour after the start, you will find that you will be the only one from the watch below not in his bunk. It may seem strange with the sun possibly still high in the summer sky, but get your head down. And now is the time when those measures you have taken to darken your berth will pay off.

Sleep.

When you are awakened, you should have your deck gear ready to hand so that you waste no time putting on oilies, harness, seaboots and sailing knife. Don't forget the calls of nature before you dress up.

It is when you go on deck now, in the dark, that everything will seem larger than life. The yacht seems to be doing 10–12 knots, the waves are twice as high as they were when you went below and the wind is blowing a near gale. This phenomenon occurs even during the relatively light summer nights of coastal waters, which paradoxically seem inky black as you peer forward and round for the first time.

Let your eyes become accustomed to the dark (it takes one minute to achieve 80 per cent adaptation; one hour to adapt fully). Find some familiar landmark or face in the cockpit. Occupy yourself in some mundane task. You will soon get used to the feeling of being in an underground train hurtling forward into a void.

Remember to keep your voice down when on night watch. Apart from waking the watch below, the owner may well be awake anyway and will almost certainly be absorbing everything you say as he lies in his bunk staring up at the deckhead. He will have the safety of his boat at heart and snatches of a few disconnected sentences such as the following will bring him on deck quicker than a rabbit flushed out by a ferret.

'. . . constant bearing . . .'

'. . . entirely unaware of our presence . . .'

'. . . a big brute too; bound to be equipped with radar'

'. . . not more than five hundred yards I'd say.'

'Nearer three.'

This is the trigger which catapults the owner from his bunk, only to discover that the crew are reminiscing about an event on the same race last year.

4
Deck Work

If you have done a bit of cruising you will probably be used to working a yacht with a relatively light crew, and you may have found yourself the strongest link; you therefore got most of the difficult jobs. You are now one of a team of strong capable men, any one of whom can do any job. In this respect, therefore, you might be tempted to consider that life will be easier.

Don't be fooled. When you were cruising, life was at a much slower tempo: the boat reefed earlier; you won't have used your spinnaker so often (and possibly not at night); all hands were available to help with the simplest manoeuvre. Offshore, despite the fact that half the crew may be on watch below, the pressure is on all the time and you must be constantly on the lookout for ways to improve speed. You won't have time to fumble, so your basic skills must be well known.

Orders

The owner will have handed command of the foredeck over to somebody else. By doing this, he also surrenders his right to direct operations from the cockpit. Even if he is tempted to tell you how to do it, you cannot hear all that shouting from the aft end, which will only distract you as you struggle with the particular task in hand. Look for your instructions from the watch leader or the foredeck chief, who will be right where the action is fastest, alongside you, and obey his orders.

Make sure that you know the meaning of any specialist words of command which may come your way. It's no good hardening a sheet when the skipper says 'check sheets' – he wants them eased. He might also use the words started or veered for the same thing. If you are told to go and hand the spinnaker staysail, nip forward and lower it, furl it, get it, don't just lay a hand on it. To muzzle a sail means to smother it when it is lowered and on deck, so that it is not blown out of control by the wind. The language is rich and varied, so don't be afraid to ask if

40

you fail to understand a command; see Appendix F for a short glossary of terms that might not be familiar to even an experienced dinghy sailer.

When you get an order, acknowledge it by repeating the instruction if you are near enough. This is a check that you are about to cast off the correct rope, or harden the right sheet. If you are some way away, lift a hand to show that you have heard quite clearly and then set about the task.

Deck Work

The essence of good deck work is a tidy ship, quick thinking and speedy action. You must play your part in keeping the boat tidy, with everything properly stowed not only where you will be able to get at it in a hurry, but where everyone else will be able to do the same. Allied to this is a sense of observation. Keep an eye open for knots coming undone, locking wire missing off a turnbuckle, a lazy halyard twisted round a stay aloft; all of these could cause a major problem later in the race if they are not corrected.

You will only be able to work quickly on deck if you feel secure. The old adage of one hand for the ship and one for yourself is all very well for the cruising man who is not in such a hurry to get there. In an offshore racer you have to give both hands to the ship if things are to be done quickly. I'm not saying that you should never hold on, but you must learn how to work freely without, at times, using a hand to steady yourself. This means that you must be hooked on in anything like brisk weather. I shall have more to say on this in the chapter on Bad Weather and Emergencies, but it is worth repeating here that you should find out what the ship's rules regarding harnesses are and obey them at all times. If you fall overboard you may lose more than the race. As a guide you can say that harnesses begin to become important as soon as the boat is moving faster than you can swim, and are vital from force 4 upwards, particularly at night or when sailing with a spinnaker – both of which will make recovery of a man overboard a more difficult process.

When handling headsails on the foredeck, sit down with your feet braced against something firm (make sure that it isn't a stowed spinnaker pole which can be forced out of its deck chocks carrying you with it). If the boat has a wire main boom preventer permanently rigged on the boom end and led along the side of the boom when not in use, make sure that it is firmly made fast at the inner end so that it may be used confidently as an extra grab wire when necessary. Get to windward of a flogging sail, or you will be covered by it as it comes down, causing you to lose balance and direction. Haul it in and trap it between your knees, but don't try and stand or kneel on it because synthetic sailcloth slips easily on itself and may carry you off your feet. Grab the foot and pull that in first, as this will help spill wind from the sail. Curl your fingers over and use the knuckles for heavy sails in wild weather, as this will be easier on the fingernails.

If there are two or more of you dealing with a headsail, one should sit forward of the stay, with his back to the pulpit, while the other helps from just aft of the stay. Never lower a sail by pulling down on the leech; you will only stretch the cloth and cause trouble later. Pull the sail down at the luff by the luffwire or luffrope; the rest will follow quickly enough.

At the mast you can sit to windward with one leg each side to give you a grip in heavy weather, thus leaving both hands for the halyard, kicking strap or what-have-you.

Hoisting

If you are hoisting sail, first check that the halyard you have got hold of is the correct one; then see how it is stowed. Check aloft to see that it is not foul round a stay or other halyard and then wait for the word of command. If possible, check visually that all is ready even when told to haul away.

Simple Halyard

A simple halyard will be a rope running to the masthead, which will belay or make fast to a cleat or belaying pin at the base of the mast. The halyard may run through a block on the end of a wire aloft, thus providing a double purchase. At all events it is brute force which brings it down and it may require two or more hands to do it. If more than two crewmen are needed, the halyard may run through a fairlead and thus along the deck; this gives room for more people to get a hold on the rope. It is important if you are hauling

42

up in a team that you all pull together, so somebody should call the time (this is the origin of many of the sea shanties sung in sailing men o' war). Having reached two blocks, or the fully hoisted point, those on the tail of the rope should be prepared for a call of 'Come up behind!' from the hand who is making fast. This means that he is ready to cleat up and needs slack in order to do so. The temptation is to fear that the sail will come down with a run if you let go, but you have to give him the slack he wants or he will never make fast with your weight on the tail; you may be sure that he is ready for the extra weight on the halyard and will be all set to whip on a holding turn as soon as he can.

Drum Winch

Fortunately the days of many hands on halyards and sheets are nearly gone for everyone, because winches can now do the job for us. A drum winch is one which takes five or six turns of rope or wire and then leaves the tail to come off the top as the halyard is winched down; the tail has to be cleated, coiled and stowed in the usual way. It is exactly like a sheet winch. To hoist a sail, haul away on the rope without bothering with the winch until you are getting near the top and the load is coming on. Five or six turns should then be put on the winch, the handle inserted securely (make sure that it's right home; a slipping handle can be dangerous and is easily lost overboard) and the final part of the hoist is then effected by the winch. When hoisting a spinnaker like this, watch out that the sail doesn't suddenly fill when half up and tear the halyard out of your hands (if it does, either the sheet hand was too quick or, more likely, you were too slow in hoisting so it serves you right). If conditions are hairy, three quarters of a turn round the winch as you hoist will not slow unduly hoisting and will keep things under control. A common form of halyard construction is to have wire tailed into rope. This allows the crew to handle the softer rope, yet leaves wire to take the strain. With the sail fully up, the wire will probably be long enough for one or two turns to lie on the drum of the winch, so that there is none of the more stretchy rope link taking the weight. When required to lower a sail which has been hoisted by a drum winch, uncleat the rope but keep tension on it, then place one hand firmly on the coils of wire round the drum and surge the halyard

43

gently so that the strain is relaxed; the turns may then be removed from the drum and the sail lowered by hand.

Reel Winch

A reel winch acts in the same way as a fishing reel, and winds the halyard (all wire in this case) onto it. Depending on its cost (and they can rise rapidly to three and even four figures), the winch may be geared for rapid early winding and slower action with more power as the sail nears the top, it will have a clutch to ease away or haul up, and will have a more or a less efficient brake to control lowering the sail. Don't rush at a strange reel winch until you have watched somebody else use it and have learned its little ways; you could inadvertently drop the mainsail with a rush. A good reel winch properly used offers complete control over the halyard, to the last inch, but it can also cut off your fingers.

Clew Outhaul

All mainsails have some control over clew outhaul tension. We have seen that there is a requirement to vary this while sailing, and some systems are easier than others.

1 LASHING   This has the advantage that it is simple and cheap. On the other hand, it is almost impossible to alter once fixed. If you are faced with one of these remember to take three or four turns round the boom as well as out to the eye at the end as you make fast, to stop the clew rising and producing wrinkles. Use knots which can be easily undone when wet.

2 WORM GEAR   The clew eye fits direct onto a sliding traveller, which is controlled by a handle often inserted into the outer end of the boom. This gives positive control but has three disadvantages: the handle can get lost; adjustment can often only be made when the boom is trimmed inboard; the various stresses set up on the worm gear and its bearings seem to promote a desire to malfunction (which is another way of saying that it doesn't always work well).

3 BLOCK AND TACKLE   The outhaul is taken over a sheave at the boom end and is then brought back towards the mast, usually inside the boom, via a system of pulleys. Adjustment is simple and positive and, because the rope comes out of the main boom near

its inner end, can be made on all points of sailing. There is often a small winch to make things easier.

Cunningham Hole

It is when hoisting sail that you will first run into the Cunningham hole so we may as well deal with it now. It will probably have to be rigged or rove or set up as the mainsail is bent on or hoisted. The hole itself will be a reinforced eye worked into the luff of the sail in question, anything from 6 to 18 inches up from the tack; it may take the form of a tab with a ring or eye in it sewn strongly into the luff. Some form of line or wire will have to be made fast to this eye, or passed through it, to a pulley system which will control its movement; each boat will vary, so leave it to somebody else the first time. At all events, see that the control line is slack when the sail goes up, or you will make life difficult as you try and hoist the last few inches against the pull of the Cunningham hole tensioner (the same goes, incidentally, for the boom downhaul and kicking strap – they must both be slack when the mainsail is hoisted). The operation of the Cunningham hole and clew outhaul are explained later.

Sheet Trimming

Sheet winches are many and varied, but they all have to be operated according to certain principles. The first and foremost of these is to take care of your fingers, because a winch can cut them off for you. Never follow a runaway rope onto the drum in a vain attempt to stop it, rather let the sail fly and lose a race than try and grip a sheet which will cost you your fingers. You will get a roasting from the watch leader for allowing the sheet to get out of control, but at least you will have four fingers left so that you can offer him two in salute when his back is turned.

A second basic principle is to remember that many winches are extremely powerful. Just because the power is available, it is not necessary to use it every time in order to grind sheets home to the last inch, particularly in light weather. Headsails should be trimmed by looking at the flow of the sail, not the final position of the clew in relation to the fairlead.

Power Ratio

All winches have a *power ratio* of some sort, or they would be of no help in pulling in a line; this is also sometimes called *mechanical advantage*. It should not be confused with *gear ratio*, which is the number of turns of the handle required to rotate the winch drum once. *Power ratio* takes account of the radius of the winch handle (and thus the leverage which can be exerted on it), the diameter of the drum (and thus the amount of line which is pulled in at each turn of the drum) and the *gear ratio* of the winch (and thus the number of turns of the winch to each turn of the handle); it can be expressed as:

$$\frac{\text{Gear ratio} \times \text{Handle radius}}{\text{Drum radius}}$$

III *Pedestal linkage* Power can be applied to either of the two big winches by use of the selector switches sited on the pedestal base. Reverse direction of the handles engages a lower gear, and there is a third gear change button on the top of each winch. *Lewmar*

Thus a winch with a 6:1 *gear ratio* using a 10 inch handle on a drum with a 2 inch radius would have a *power ratio* of 30:1. If the drum radius were increased to 3 inches, the power ratio would drop to 20:1, but half as much rope again would be pulled in at each turn of the handle (although it would be half as hard again to work). A simple winch with a 1:1 gear ratio (i.e. no gearing at all, hence the drum turns at the same speed as the handle) and a radius of $1\frac{1}{2}$ inches could be given a *power ratio* or *mechanical advantage* of 100:1 if you were to use a ridiculously long handle of 12 ft 6 in. What you as a crewman have to remember is that it is easy to overstretch certain sails (light weather headsails made of light cloth) by harsh use of powerful winches. A powerful winch can be recognised not only by its size and the ease with which it does its job, but also by its slow speed of rotation when geared down.

Finally, don't haul on the standing part of the sheet in front of the winch or you will get a riding turn, and beware of some winches with tapered barrels which cause the turns on the drum to slide up or down and pinch unwary fingers. If the sheet goes aft to a block first and then forward to the winch, don't go and stand in the vee thus created, in case of failure of the block or its shackle.

Types of Winch

There are several basic types of winch. At the top end of the scale (by size, power and price) is the so-called coffee grinder. This is a capstan type winch operated by two vertically rotating opposed handles on a pedestal, and it generates enormous power (it takes two crewmen to work it). There is then the top action winch, where the handle fits into a recess in the top of the drum and can be turned through 360 degrees; the bottom action winch has a handle at the base of the drum which works on a backwards and forwards ratchet principle (the drum of this type is always free to put on turns of rope as there is no handle in the way, but the ratchet action is slower than turning the handle a complete circle); the under-deck winch has a handle which protrudes under the deck directly below the centre of the winch and it can thus be turned through 360 degrees, yet does not hinder putting turns of the sheet on the drum. Finally, two or more top action winches can be linked to the coffee-grinder, to remote action cranking points (molehills) or together, so that cranking at one point turns a winch elsewhere.

Gear Changing

When a winch is geared down, it usually has two or sometimes three speeds. Changing gear can be effected by altering the direction of turning the handle – usually clockwise gives direct drive (1:1) and anti-clockwise gives the gearing, be it 4:1, 6:1 or whatever (the winch drum, of course, continues to rotate in the same direction, usually clockwise, when the handle is reversed, but it turns at a slower speed in low gear). Another type of gear change is by lever, while the handle continues to be turned in its original direction. Three speed winches usually employ a combination of both these systems.

IV *Self-tailing winches* The helmsman can tack the boat single handed when using self-tailing winches. The sheet feeds round the groove at the top of the drum and is eased away when it reaches the lever which is facing the camera. *Lewmar*

Cleats

Before we look a little more closely at particular types of winches, it is worth saying a few words about sheet cleats. These can be of three main types and, whatever type is used, it should be sited clear of the

48

radius of the winch handle and on the opposite side of the winch to the fairlead. In this way the winchman will not bark his knuckles on the cleat as he turns the handle and the strain on the sheet acts either side of the winch, so the pull of the two parts of the rope cancels out when the sheet is cleated.

1 CONVENTIONAL TWO HORNED CLEAT   The sheet is made fast by a round turn followed by figure of eight turns, usually without a half hitch to finish off with, so that it can be thrown off in a hurry without trouble. The two horns should make an angle between 15–20 degrees with the natural run of the rope as it comes off the winch; in this way the round turn can be taken without jamming under the horns or on itself.

2 WEDGE SHAPED JAM CLEAT   This has a snub end opposite the wedge, and the cleat should again make an angle between 15–20 degrees with the rope as it comes off the winch, with the wedge pointing towards the winch. The sheet is first taken round the snub end and then jammed under the wedge; there should be no need for a second turn or a figure of eight.

3 CLAMSHELL TYPE CLEAT   This should point directly along the line of the rope, and it operates by laying the sheet directly into the jaws of the clam.

Coffee Grinders

You may sail for a long time without meeting a coffee grinder winch. This is a large and powerful piece of machinery, and takes two men to work it on opposite sides of a pedestal. It will have some sort of gear change system and it may be linked with another coffee grinder. The rope will probably cleat direct to the top of the drum. If you meet one, you are on a very big and expensive yacht (one coffee grinder can cost as much as a secondhand aircraft) with plenty of expert company to show you how to work it, so I won't go further into this particular form of sail torture here.

Pedestal Drive

As mentioned briefly above, several winches can be linked together or to one central pedestal. The pedestal is a form of coffee grinder, but without its own drum; it can therefore be sited where one or two men can bring full power to bear. As with two linked winches,

49

the power input is out of the way of the operating drum, so that the man calling the trim can work unobstructed. There will be both a gear change lever and a selector switch to link the drive to the appropriate drum.

Molehills

These are remote drive points for a single horizontally rotating handle, so that power may be applied away from the winch itself. The socket is faired into the deck so that it does not cause an obstruction. There is usually an isolating switch, so that drive may be coupled or disconnected at will.

Linked winches confer two principal advantages. First they free the drum onto which the sheet is wound from obstruction of the handle at the top. Secondly they enable the man cranking to be both out of the way of the driven winch and up to windward, where his weight is usually better placed. The power input may be at the top of another winch, at a pedestal or via a molehill.

Top Action Winches

The most usual form of winch construction on offshore racers is the top action. Before using any winch, check the direction of rotation of the drum. Most of them go clockwise, but there are those boats which have handed winches, that is to say they rotate in opposite directions on opposite sides of the cockpit: outwards or inwards, usually the former. To avoid the danger of a riding turn (one turn of rope caught under another on the drum) it is usually best to take only two turns on the drum while hauling in relatively slack sheet (none at all if there is no danger of the line snatching away, as in the early stages of hoisting a sail which has a halyard winch, or in very light weather). When the strain comes on, take a total of 4 or 5 turns according to how many turns the winch will accommodate and also the strength of the wind (more turns will hold better) and then put in the handle. What happens often is that the man with the handle puts it in the socket too quickly, and the man on the sheet has to shout at him.

'Wait a second! Let me get another turn on the drum.'

Usually one man will work the handle while another tails on the line, and there is one principal mistake which each can make. The former should not fit his handle before the tailer has got all the

50

V *Winching* One man tails while another winds. This crewman has a foot in the vee formed by the line, which is bad in principle: if anything gives he could get a nasty injury.
Lewmar

turns he needs on the drum and the latter should not be so eager when tacking that he backs the headsail by hauling in too soon. You should try and harden sheet as much as you can while the headsail is flapping head to wind; under certain circumstances you can sheet right home without having to winch at all (much depends on the helmsman and the speed at which he puts the boat in stays), which all helps to lessen the work load. But be careful not to pull in too soon, or you will backwind the sail or snag the leech on the foredeck. Normally it will be necessary to hand haul first, winch the easy part in high gear and then change to low gear for the final inches.

Bottom Action Winches

A bottom action winch has a lever semi-permanently fitted at the base of the drum. The idea is that turns can be put on and taken off without disturbing the handle. To work the winch, however, requires a backwards and forwards ratchet movement of the handle which is limited in its operation to a quadrant of the winch's radius. This is a slow procedure and there is seldom any gearing for these winches, which are thus strictly limited in their usefulness to small boats or at least small loadings.

Under Deck Action Winches

In order to be able to put turns of rope on the drum without removing a handle, which can yet turn through 360 degrees, there are winches which operate via a handle which projects downwards. The winch is usually mounted near the cockpit coaming and the handle is turned under the side deck. Deep cockpit walls make this type of limited application, however, as the handle shaft has then to be too long for efficient use.

Self-tailing Winches

Self-tailing winches hold the tail of the sheet fast in a toothed groove as it comes off the top of the drum. This takes up the slack as the winch is rotated, the extreme tail being automatically eased out of the groove as it reaches a special release lever.

General Precautions

As I said just now, always check the direction of rotation of the

VI *Riding turns* If a riding turn is allowed to develop, later turns of the sheet will ride up on top of it. This can become very difficult to clear under load. *Author*

VII *Easing sheets* Note how the cupped palm of the hand is placed flat on the full width of the turns when the sheet is eased. Control is then maintained by easing the free end of the sheet with the right hand to slacken it, and by pressing the turns firmly round the drum with the palm of the left hand to hold them steady and stop them going out in jerks. *Author*

VIII *Casting off a sheet* To cast a sheet off a winch, the turns should be uncoiled from above. This avoids tangles and keeps fingers out of harm's way. *Author*

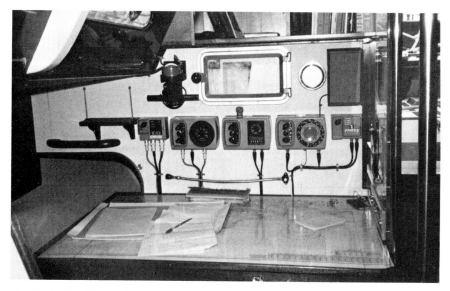

IX *Chart table* The navigator's compartment in *Quailo*. Note the opening window so that he can both see and speak to the cockpit. The top of the chart table is Perspex with a chart spread underneath it. *Author*

X *Winch battery* A battery of winches at the base of a mast, backed up by horn cleats each angled at about 20 degrees to its respective winch. *Lewmar*

drum before putting turns on a strange winch. Make sure that the handle is properly fitted before using it, for they can flick overboard easily (and they are surprisingly expensive items). *Never* leave the handle in an unattended winch, but be careful to stow it properly where the next man will find it quickly. *Never* put a winch handle down loose on deck, even for a second, if you don't want a sudden lurch of the boat to lose it overboard. *Never* pull a line in front of a winch or you will get a riding turn. Watch out for your fingers. Check that you know how to work the brake before lowering a sail on a reel halyard winch.

Easing Sheets

If you are given the order to check or ease a sheet which is on a winch, take it off the cleat but keep the strain pulling against the winch with the other hand, so that you don't let it run with a sudden surge. Place the free hand with the palm cupped round the turns of rope on the winch so that you can hold them firmly against the drum. You will now find that you can ease as much or as little as you like by combined action of your two hands. If you are required to cast off, once again take the line off the cleat but keep the strain. At the appropriate moment (when tacking, usually as the headsail starts to lift, which will not be until the boat has swung about 15–20 degrees), lift the line well above the winch, uncoiling it from the drum with a rising corkscrew motion of the hand. This makes sure that the turns are taken off without snarling up and that your fingers are well out of harm's way.

Riding Turns

To get rid of a riding turn which will not pull free, load must be taken off the sheet as it approaches the winch. This means one of three things.

1 Pull the sheet in by hand from the wrong side of the winch.
2 Set up a jury sheet to take the strain, and haul it tighter than the jammed sheet.
3 Rig a relieving tackle, using a rolling hitch or a Tarbuck knot (see Chapter 9), on the standing part of the jammed sheet where it leads to the drum, and take the strain.

5
Theory of Sail

Some of you will know already that I am interested in problems connected with sails. It may not surprise you, therefore, to find this chapter in a book on crewing.

To my mind it needs no defence or explanation but, to those who may think that it does, I would suggest that it is of little use talking about trim of sails until we agree what we are striving to achieve and, more important, why.

What then is the object of a sail trim? Briefly it is so to adjust the sails of a boat that, between them, they provide the most efficient conversion of the wind into forward speed. To find out how to do this we must first know how the sails turn energy into speed.

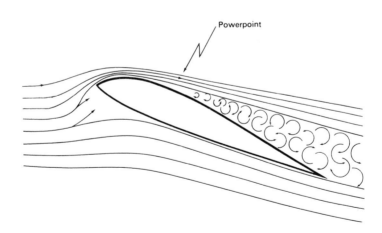

3 *Aerofoil at 25 degrees in a slow airstream* The upper streamlines break away from the surface just aft of the powerpoint. From there aft, the air is turbulent and reverts to normal atmospheric pressure. Streamlines which are close together show higher speed together with lower pressure, and *vice versa*. There is thus high pressure beneath the aerofoil and low pressure above it.

Aerodynamics

They do it of course by producing thrust in much the same way that an aircraft's wing produces lift. Imagine a wing at the fairly broad angle of attack of 25 degrees in a slow moving airstream; figure 3 shows the airflow round such a wing. You can see how the stream-lines break away from the upper surface at about the halfway position.

The streamlines which show movement of the air also indicate its relative speed: where they are close together the speed is greater and, conversely, it is slower where they are further apart. It will be seen that airspeed above the wing is greater than that below it.

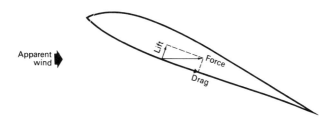

4 *Lift and drag* High pressure on the underside of an aerofoil pushes the aerofoil upwards. Skin friction and other forms of drag tend to hold it back. The parallelogram of forces can be crudely resolved as shown. There are similar forces on the upper surface.

Lift

We know that pressure varies with wind speed: the faster the speed the lower the pressure and *vice versa*. It follows that pressure is lower above the wing and higher below it; this gives rise to a tendency for the wing to move upwards: *lift*. In addition, the energy required to deflect the wind from its original path has, in obedience to Newton's Law, and equal and opposite reaction on the wing up-wards (more lift). These forces can be resolved at right angles to the surface (lift) and parallel to it (drag); see fig. 4.

We can now skip several intermediate stages of multiple small arrows showing the breakdown of lift generated by these different contributions and we get a single arrow showing the combined force of all these effects.

Powerpoint

It will be seen from figure 5 that this force acts slightly forward of a right angle to the main chord of the wing and near to the position of maximum camber. This position of maximum camber will come into the discussion fairly often and is rather a mouthful. A shorter description would help us all and, in my book *Dinghy Sails,* I have adopted the word 'powerpoint' in default of anything better; I shall use it throughout this chapter.

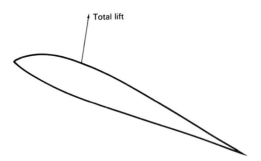

5   *Total lift* If the lift from the upper surface of the aerofoil is added to that produced by the lower surface, we get a total resultant lift force which can be shown by one arrow. This shows the relative strength (by its length), and direction of the force. It usually acts just forward of right angles to the chord from a position near the powerpoint.

We can now substitute a sail for our wing and get a similar airflow pattern. The wind flows faster round the upper, or leeward, side; it generates lift or thrust in a similar fashion to the wing, as shown in figure 6. It will be seen that the streamlines break away from the surface of both the wing and the sail just aft of the power-point. When this happens, pressure immediately returns to normal in the turbulence, thus cutting down the low pressure which we want to encourage to leeward in order to get more thrust.

Slot

In an aircraft's wing, this turbulence can be delayed by introducing a slot into the aerofoil, in order to revitalise the flow over the upper surface through bleeding off some of the slower moving high press-ure air from the other side.

Figure 7 shows the effect on the streamlines when this is done. Notice how the onset of turbulence is now delayed past the power-

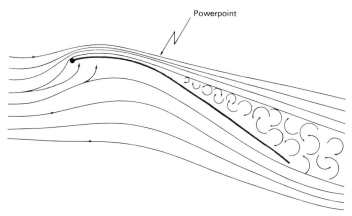

6 *Airflow round a sail* Compare the flow round a single sail closehauled, unsupported by a headsail, with that round an aerofoil without a slot. Note again how the streamlines to leeward break away just aft of the powerpoint, leaving turbulent air over a large part of the sail, which is thus not contributing any thrust.

point and towards the trailing edge; this is the principle of the slot acting in front of a high lift flap. Once again we can substitute sails for our wing and we can at last see where all this is getting us.

Single Aerofoil

We now have a mainsail and headsail acting in concert to produce a smooth airflow round a *single* aerofoil (fig. 8). It is important always to think of these two sails as a single unit, with a slot between them, and not as two separate aerofoils.

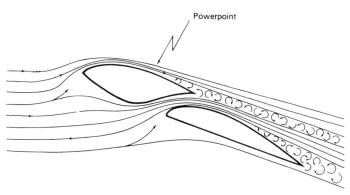

7 *Slot effect on an aerofoil* If a slot is introduced into an aerofoil which is at or near the stall, the leeward streamlines are cleaned up and the stall delayed, with resulting increase in lift.

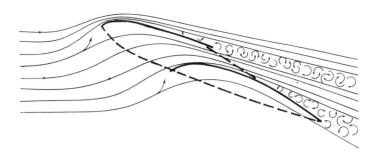

8 *Slot effect on sails* Introduction of a headsail in front of a mainsail in the closehauled condition immediately cleans up the airflow to leeward, thus providing more thrust. This diagram has been drawn so that the aerofoil formed by both sails is the same size as the aerofoil in fig. 7 and the sail in fig. 6. Note how the streamlines are less turbulent aft of the powerpoint, with resulting better performance.

The slot is all-important in this aerodynamic situation, due to its beneficial effect on the leeward airflow. If the slot is too convergent or there is too much overlap, air will build up in the narrow neck, backwind the mainsail and create the very turbulence we are trying to avoid, as shown in figure 9. A narrow slot, with considerable overlap, can be accepted at slow wind speeds because we are then dealing with small volumes of air; as the wind strength increases so must the slot become larger to allow more air to pass through; this is one of the reasons for changing to a smaller headsail at high wind speeds.

A similar condition will be created by a headsail with a bellied leech which directs the wind straight into the lee side of the mainsail. These are two situations, therefore, which should be avoided.

If, on the other hand, you have too wide a gap between the two sails, you get a breakdown of the single aerofoil which we have seen is desirable, and the sails revert to being two mutually interfering aerofoils, each with its own turbulent air to leeward; see fig. 10.

It has, in fact, been shown in wind tunnel tests at the University of Southampton that the leech of a headsail should at least reach the powerpoint of its mainsail for maximum efficiency to be achieved in the close-hauled condition. Further, the airflow at the exit to the slot should be parallel with the lee side of the mainsail.

The trim of headsail and mainsail, therefore, is a nice exercise in judgement to see that the headsail provides the guiding hand to improve the leeward streamlines in the way we know it can.

61

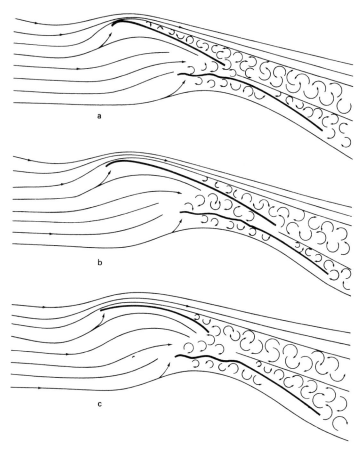

9 *Poor slot effect* If the wind cannot flow smoothly between the headsail and the mainsail it will bunch in the slot, become turbulent before it passes to the leeward side, and thus fail to revitalise the leeward flow.

(a) The headsail sheet is led too far inboard, thus closing the gap. This may be all right for light winds, when not much air is trying to pass through, but quickly becomes too narrow as the volume of air increases at higher wind speeds.
(b) There is too much overlap here, thus effectively closing the gap again.
(c) A bellied headsail leech deflects the wind onto the lee side of the mainsail.

Successful boats these days will usually number a specialist sail trimmer in the crew. Thus, those of you who do not have the brawn to work the coffee grinder or the experience to take the helm, may instead take heart. Examine the finer points of aerodynamics as applied to sails and learn how to conjure up an extra half knot by careful trimming.

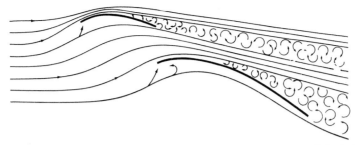

10 *Slot too open* If headsail and mainsail are separated too much, a good deal of the slot effect is lost and both sails revert to acting independently. Each stalls at or near its powerpoint and the powerful effect which the headsail can have is largely dissipated, with resulting loss of thrust.

Telltales

Laminar flow over the combined aerofoil is important, particularly at the luff of the headsail, which is the leading edge, because any turbulence at this point will disturb the whole flow pattern. Telltales at the genoa luff are simple and effective in revealing whether this desirable state of affairs exists; on the mainsail they should be placed at the powerpoint, to show whether the headsail is doing its job of delaying separation of the streamlines properly. If a windward telltale does not stream nicely along the surface of the sail, either the boat should be turned away from the wind or the sail sheeted harder, and *vice versa* for leeward telltales. My mnemonic for the man who always gets it wrong is TASTES: Turn Away or Sheet Towards Erratic Streamers.

Thrust

It is not my intention here to go too deeply into the parallelogram of forces, with explanations of lift and drag (you should consult my book *Sails* if you want to know more about this). But you do need to understand a bit about forward thrust and heeling moment because, if you can increase the former and/or decrease the latter, you will add to the forward speed of the boat. We are not concerned with how sails develop thrust so much as how we can help them work to best efficiency. Let us therefore now turn to a mainsail which is close-hauled at say, five degrees to the fore and aft line of the boat.

Total force can be resolved into forward thrust and heeling moment as shown in figure 11. If you now allow the boom angle to alter by five degrees to leeward, with all other factors staying the same, first see that the sail remains full and does not allow the wind to get behind it and cause the luff to lift. Assuming the sail stays full and the total force (or wind strength) remains the same, you will get a considerable increase in forward thrust and a lessening of heeling moment as the total force is angled more towards the way you are trying to go. You are converting more wind power along your course and less across it: more thrust, less heel.

It has been established under test conditions that headsail trim has more effect on a boat's speed than adjustment of the main boom but there is, nevertheless, a science to the latter which should also be understood.

In light weather and smooth water you can afford to bring the main boom well into the middle of the boat, so that you point higher and make ground to windward. If you are doing this, the

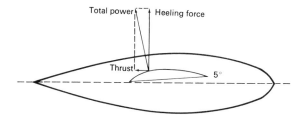

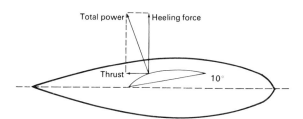

11 *Sail trim, closehauled* If a mainsail can be eased from an angle of 5 degrees to the centreline to 10 degrees without lifting or requiring an alteration of course, the result is a minor decrease in heeling force and a dramatic increase in thust by as much as 50 per cent. This takes no account of heading when beating to windward, and the closer sheeting position may, of course, pay through an ability to point higher: much will depend on wind strength and sea conditions.

64

headsail lead should also be brought further inboard by barberhauling. In strong winds it is better to have the genoa sheeted further outboard to open the slot and allow a greater volume of air to pass through the venturi. When it gets really strong, the main boom can also be eased along the traveller, so that the wind escapes from the leech without acting as too much of a heeling moment or brake, but you should have a smaller headsail in order to maintain the open slot. The main traveller can also be eased with advantage in the more disturbed waters which you will meet offshore, where it is usually better to sail the boat a little more free and push her through the seas.

Sail Camber

We now come to the question of camber. How much belly should a sail have under given conditions and why? This is different from the basic angle of the sail to the fore and aft line, such as is produced by easing or hardening the main boom and, on the mainsail, is achieved by use of various sail controls which we shall examine below.

Heavy weather needs flat sails while light weather needs full ones. This is a fundamental principle which holds good for most conditions, but which may need qualification in particular circumstances.

Controls

Before we go any further we should find out what control we have over the shape of the sails when they are in use. To understand this, we must first know what happens to sailcloth when it has wind pressure in it.

All woven sailcloth stretches. The practical effect of this is that the powerpoint of a sail is pushed aft towards the leech as the wind increases. Its position is also affected if tension is put on the cloth to stretch it in one direction: the cloth will compensate by contracting in another. Thus, if tension is put on the luff of a sail to elongate it on the hoist, the sail will contract across its chord and draw the leech towards the luff. This will remove cloth from the leech area, flatten the sail and cause more flow at the luff. This applies not only

65

to mainsails but also to headsails, if the latter are made so that luff tension can be varied. For the first half of this century headsails were made with luffs permanently seized to wires, after the sail-maker had pulled the cloth by an arbitrary amount which he decided was enough to give correct flow for average conditions. This permanent seizing meant that flow could not be varied to suit different wind strengths, so the sail in question could not be correctly cambered for one set of conditions. Nowadays most headsails either have a rope or tape luff, exactly like a mainsail, or else the sail is sleeved over a wire (which is longer than the unstretched sailcloth) and adjusted by pulling down on the tack be means of a suitable tensioning arrangement.

Halyard

The most obvious control we have is the halyard which, as we have seen, draws flow from the middle or aft part of the sail gradually towards the luff as greater tension is put on it and the cloth is contracted across the line of tension. A basic principle to adopt when hoisting a mainsail is never to be a slave to the black bands painted on the spars. When racing you must not, of course, hoist the sail so that it goes beyond the black bands at any point, but you do not have to pull until it reaches the mark just because some rule maker has caused it to be put there. Nevertheless, increasing use of Cunningham holes and mast bend has meant that most mainsails nowadays do in fact go easily up to the mark at the masthead, so that further flattening is effected by alternative means.

Clew Outhaul

The clew outhaul of a mainsail controls the shape of the very important area just over the boom. This is a vital part of the sail because it offers the largest area for every foot of the luff, thus producing more forward thrust than an equivalent slice nearer to the head, but it also has less heeling moment because it is low down. Develop thrust in the sail low down, therefore, and you will be a long way towards an efficient aerofoil. Easing the clew will produce more camber; tightening it will flatten the whole of the area over the boom. Most racing boats have a jiffy reef incorporated along the foot, for use with or without a Cunningham hole, to flatten the sail in this area as the wind increases.

Headsail Sheet

For the first few inches of its travel from the hard in position, a headsail sheet acts in the same way as the mainsail clew outhaul on the sail's camber: it develops flow along the foot. It then goes on to ease the sail sideways as the boat comes further off the wind.

Mainsheet Traveller

Because it has no effect on the tension of the sailcloth, the mainsheet traveller does not alter the camber of the mainsail when used in close hauled conditions. I have included it here in order to make it clear that it is not a control as far as basic sail camber is concerned, but is only used to alter the angle of the sail to the wind relative to the fore and aft line of the boat and to cut down twist. It has considerable effect on weather helm, and many boats, particularly those of light displacement, are sailed to windward with one hand on the main traveller to help balance the rig.

Cunningham Hole

Named after its inventor Briggs Cunningham, who developed it in the 6-metre days, the Cunningham hole is a simple and cheap way of controlling flow at the forward end of a sail. It consists of an eye worked into the luff anything from 6–18 inches up from the tack, depending on the size of the sail. A line passed through this hole can then apply tension downwards on the luff, thus stretching further a sail which has already been pulled to its maximum on the halyard. A mainsail or genoa may therefore be made to maximum size for use in medium winds. When the wind gets up and blows the camber aft into the leech, the flow needs to be drawn forward again by applying further tension to the luff. This cannot be achieved through the halyard, because the head of the sail is already as high as it will go. It is therefore applied by means of pulling down on the Cunningham hole. The result is a series of radiating creases in the tack area, but these are a small price to pay for a far better overall shape of the sail in question caused by the extra luff tension. The system has two prime requirements: it must be permanently rigged so that it can be operated at any time; it must have some sort of purchase (tackle or winch) in order to get sufficient pull.

Mast Bend

Mast bend needs a so-called fractional rig to work to best effect. That is to say, the forestay should attach to the mast below the truck some $\frac{3}{4}$ or $\frac{7}{8}$ths of the way up from the deck; but it can still be effected on a masthead rig through use of an adjustable babystay to draw the lower part of the mast forward when it is tensioned. In any kind of a lop or seaway it is best to have running backstays, which should be set up hand tight to steady the rig.

Bending the mast flattens the mainsail, by allowing the luff to bow forward and take out some of the extra cloth built into that part of the sail to help give fullness. This in turn reduces heel, eases

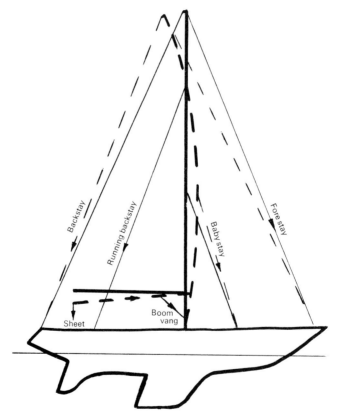

12 *Mast bend* Bending the mast does not move the centre of effort a great deal, but it flattens the mainsail. A variety of stresses are set up in the rig as shown.

weather helm and slackens the leech, thus allowing the wind to escape – all good things if they are not carried to excess.

Mast Rake

If mast rake can be changed by adjustment of the backstay and forestay, the centre of effort will be shifted in relation to the centre of lateral resistance (but beware, for the IOR has something to say about the legality of this while racing). This is of prime importance when considering the broach, as we shall see later, because it alters the force couple which is trying to make the boat turn about its point of pivot.

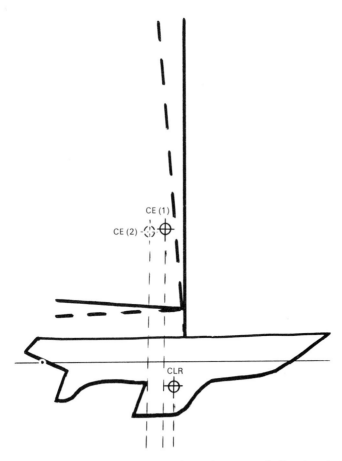

13 *Mast rake* Raking the mast moves the dynamic centre of effort in relation to the centre of lateral resistance. This affects the force couple and the amount of weather helm.

So effective is raking the mast forward in reducing weather helm, that there is a danger that the crew will not appreciate the full strength of the wind. The boat is well balanced, so she must be going to best effect. However, she may well be heeling so much that her resulting underwater asymmetry is causing excessive drag; the time to reef has arrived.

Kicking Strap and Topping Lift

The kicking strap or boom vang only controls twist in a mainsail and does not alter its basic camber. It should be fairly tight to eliminate twist when the boat is off the wind, because this means that the lower half of the mainsail can be eased further off without causing the head to backwind or lift; you are getting more thrust and less heel.

If the kicking strap is not formed by a hydraulic ram or wheel tensioned rod which can be extended to force the boom upwards, its opposite control is the topping lift, and there are special circumstances of light winds when it can pay to hoist the boom a little to give a better angle to the sail aloft.

Where a boat has a tendency to broach easily, it is important to be able to slacken the kicking strap quickly in order to induce twist, so that heeling pressure is dumped from the top of the mainsail; we shall discuss this further shortly. A spring-loaded vang will help this.

Hydraulics

Before leaving controls, we must briefly look at the hydraulics which are frequently incorporated into their functioning.

Hydraulics confer terrific power which is, moreover, easily controlled and, furthermore, measurable. Installations vary from a pump operating on the backstay alone, to complex arrangements whereby power can be switched between backstay, forestay, babystay, kicking strap and mast partners. Great care is needed in operating such a system to ensure that stays which are not required to be altered are isolated. I recall sailing a One-Tonner when a keen new arrival in the crew leaped to harden the backstay as we rounded the leeward mark to come on the wind. The rest of the crew were too busy to pay him much attention and, in any case, he had come with a good reputation and was clearly doing the right thing. What nobody noticed until too late was that he had not isolated the other outputs so, while he was tightening the backstay, he was also trying to extend the kicking strap. But the main sheet was by now hard in and, such is the force of hydraulic power, he bent the kicker ram rather expensively.

The moral is to learn the system thoroughly before you start playing with it.

Drawstring

If the halyard draws flow forward, it follows that tension on the leech will draw it aft. This can be useful under conditions of reaching and running, where you want the flow right aft. Some reaching headsails have a second drawstring running from tack to clew in order to curl the foot into a bag when off the wind.

Having seen what controls are available to us, we can now examine what action is needed both close-hauled and free in various wind conditions. If we look at the mainsail because it has more controls, we can also assume that the same principles hold good for headsails.

Close-hauled

Light Weather

In light weather there will not be enough wind to blow out of shape the camber so carefully tailored into the sail by the sailmaker. It should be hoisted, therefore, with little tension so that there is a smooth curve with its powerpoint about half way back from the luff towards the leech. In practice, the mainsail is either hoisted until the headboard is on its mark at the masthead, the boom is then raised or lowered until the correct flow is obtained; or those boats with a fixed gooseneck adjust the halyard to get the same result (and they will have a suitably powerful halyard winch to enable them to do this). Similar principles go for the clew, which should be eased well forward until a large and even camber is achieved; headsail sheets are not tightened so hard that the sail is pulled flat along the foot (this is usually revealed in practice by the foot of the jib bearing hard against the shroud, or the upper leech being pulled against the spreader end). The mainsheet traveller should be amidships so that the boat will point high; ease it in a seaway because she

71

will probably go better if she is pushed through it a bit more. In the smooth conditions found inshore, the boat will point higher if the main boom is hauled up to windward on the traveller and the genoa is barberhauled inboard.

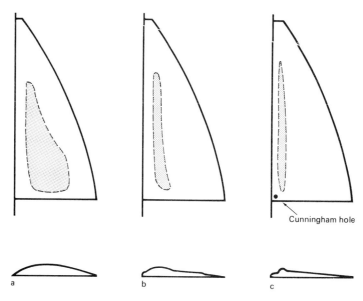

14 *Flow or camber* A sail should be hoisted according to wind strength. These illustrations show the shapes of a mainsail with the boat at rest. In light weather there will not be enough wind to change the shape of (a), so it should not be hoisted hard enough to draw any of the flow forward; medium weather will cause a slight shift in flow towards the leech, so enough tension is put on the luff to cause the beginnings of a fold to appear as in (b); the flow which has been induced in the form of a hard fold up the luff of (c) will be blown well aft by heavy weather, so not only should there be plenty of tension put on the halyard, but the Cunningham hole should also be pulled down.

Medium Weather

As the wind increases, so should the luff and foot be tensioned, so that the flow is brought towards the luff and the lower part of the sail flattened (but beware of tensioning the foot too much, leaving the sail as flat as a board; you want flow and drive low down). As soon as the wind blows into the sail, this flow will be increased and pushed aft, so you should put enough tension on the halyard to cause the beginnings of a fold to appear up the luff when the boat is head to wind. The mainsheet traveller may now be eased slightly to leeward if the sea is rough, but don't overdo it. The Cunningham hole should not be needed yet; keep the leechline slack.

Heavy Weather

Now is the time when the mainsail should be pulled right to its black bands and the headsail hoisted as hard as it will go, using full tension on halyard and, in the case of the mainsail, outhaul. When sails are fully hoisted, harsh use of the Cunningham hole will be necessary in really strong winds. The result may look odd before you fill away on a tack, but the wind will soon change all that. The mainsheet traveller should be eased all the way, so that the wind flows off the sail and does not brake the boat by catching hold of a hard leech. Mainsail and headsail sheets should be pulled in hard. Ease any leechline which may have been tightened to control a drumming leech. You must take a more than usually critical look at the shape of both sails individually and together (our combined aerofoil again) to see that you have achieved as undisturbed a flow as possible. Bend the mast by putting tension on the babystay and take in the flattening reef along the foot of the mainsail. The helmsman will feel the effect on the amount of weather helm he has, and will call for successive measures as the wind increases – clew, traveller, Cunningham, flattening reef, mast bend.

Off the Wind

It is a fair generalisation to say that you need to ease all sail controls, except the kicking strap and leechline when running. The shape of sail now required is a baggy one, which will convert wind power into thrust better when off the wind. It is for this reason that some mainsails are fitted with a zipper or jiffy reef along the foot: when it is opened the sail is given a great deal more flow low down and becomes a better shape for reaching and running (and for windward work in light weather). If the mainsail tack is allowed to rise, the clew to go forward and the traveller to run down to leeward, the desired shape is achieved. Ease the headsail halyard if the sail has a rope or tape luff, and also the sheet to get the same result; if the regular fairlead is inboard, it should be barberhauled as far out towards the toerail as it will go, and slightly aft. Needless to say, the Cunningham hole should be relaxed if it has been pulled down.

Kicking Strap

The kicking strap should be kept tight on a reach, so that the boom is pulled down to eliminate twist. If the boat does not have a solid kicker in the shape of a hydraulic ram or wheel tensioned bar, it may be found that the permanent gear cannot do the job properly due to poor mechanical advantage, so a boom vang must be rigged. This usually takes the form of a webbing strap which runs from the boom to a strong-point on the deck or toerail, tension being applied through a tackle.

Leechline

As I said earlier, the leechline can be used to advantage off the wind. If it is pulled down it will cause the aft part of the sail to bag, but care must be taken to see that it is not overdone on a shy or close reach. The wind needs to be aft of the beam for its use to be profitable.

Topping Lift

In light winds extra flow can sometimes be given to the mainsail by raising the boom a foot or so on the topping lift, or by extending the solid kicking strap. This, in fact, imparts twist to the sail, but this does not matter at the light wind speeds we are considering; what we are after is a baggy shape, particularly aloft where there might be more wind (which incidentally will be at a slightly greater angle due to wind gradient, particularly if the boat is $\frac{3}{4}$ rigged, where the upper wind is not deflected to a finer angle by the genoa).

Broaching

Before we leave this chapter on theory, I would like to say a few words on broaching and what can be done to help minimise it.

When a boat is sailing close-hauled, her centre of lateral resistance or plane under water (CLR) is usually acting through a point a short distance in front of the centre of effort of her sails (CE); this is the dynamic situation, although statically the reverse may be the case. She thus has a tendency to pivot under the influence of this force couple and point into wind. This is weather helm, and we have all experienced it in a well balanced boat – indeed, three

74

or four degrees of weather helm is said to give a better hydro-dynamic flow over the keel and thus is no bad thing. When the boat is heeling on a spinnaker reach, however, two things happen to upset this desirable state of affairs.

First, the CE shifts to leeward as the boat heels, thus offsetting it further from the CLR to increase the force couple. Secondly, the spinnaker has a tendency to bury the bow (it pulls from the mast-head as well as the sheet and guy, so it is not quite the lifting force it is sometimes made out to be). This puts more wetted area into the water forward, so that the CLR moves forward (further still from the CE); see fig 15. This is aggravated by the fact that the rudder lifts out of the water, thus not only reducing lateral area aft still more, but also drastically reducing the effect of the rudder as the helmsman struggles to maintain a straight course.

Where a boat has a long keel, with a lot of wetted area when upright, the extra immersion of the lee bow will not make such a large percentage change in the CLR as it will if the lateral area is small in the first place. Two or three extra square feet will not radically shift the centre of a hundred square feet, but they will have an appreciable effect on a total of only thirty square feet or so. This is why fin and skeg boats have a greater tendency to broach than their long keeled sisters. Light displacement boats with very short keels or dagger plates can broach so viciously that the truck goes right down to the water – so-called tip trucking. It is a price which sometimes has to be paid in return for the ability to plane exhilarat-ingly at remarkable speeds of 20 knots or so. But the crew should be aware when the boat is in a critical condition, and thus be alert for early symptoms of a spectacular gyration. Skilful trimming can often avert trouble, but action has to be swift and sure.

Preventive Measures

Preventive measures are clear: restrict heeling to a minimum and stop the bow going down. Easier said than done sometimes, but careful playing of the spinnaker and mainsail can work wonders.

Make sure that the thrust from the spinnaker is as much forward as possible; too much sideways power will cause the boat to heel excessively, and the aft part of the sail may well be actively pulling astern to nullify some of the drive you think you are getting. Keep the pole aft and ease the sheet as much as possible (the situation is

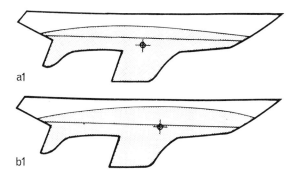

a1

b1

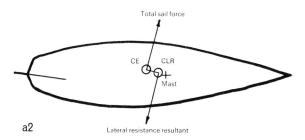

Total sail force

CE   CLR

Mast

a2   Lateral resistance resultant

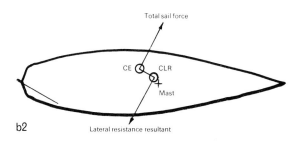

Total sail force

CE   CLR

Mast

b2   Lateral resistance resultant

15 *Broaching* When the average fin and skeg boat is close hauled in force 3–4, she heels to the wind and has a centre of lateral resistance as shown in (a) (1). If a spinnaker is hoisted on a close reach, the boat heels more and the bow is depressed; this shifts the CLR forward as in (b) (1). The plan views of these two conditions are shown at (a) (2) and (b) (2) respectively, where the centre of effort has moved sideways as the boat heels, and the moment arm is increased further by the shift forward of the CLR. Note the greater rudder angle of (b) (2), trying to overcome the bigger force couple with only semi-immersion.

The best cure lies in prevention. Keep heeling to a minimum and stop the bow going down. If this fails, the forces involved must be reduced by dumping wind from the mainsail and/or collapsing the spinnaker.

76

different on a dead run, where rhythmic rolling can cause a broach due to aggravation of the disturbing effect on the balance of forces caused by the quarter wave. This calls for the spinnaker sheet to be hardened more than normal and taken forward in order to control the roll). Some boats prefer to use the double head rig of genoa and staysail when the wind is forward of the beam, because this eliminates the rear component of thrust and the bow down tendency produced by a shy spinnaker, thus effectively preventing the broach.

Being well aft, thrust from the mainsail is a major factor in the fore and aft location of the CE. To start with, the direction in which the mainsail drives is strongly affected by the degree to which the sail is allowed to twist. A lot of twist means that, in order to keep the upper part of the sail drawing, the lower part is further inboard than desirable, thus pushing too much sideways. Reduce twist and the boom can be eased, thrust is more forward, heel is reduced and the CE less widely separated from the CLR.

In order to help keep the rudder in the water and the boat as upright as possible, bring the crew well aft and to windward.

Corrective Action

Despite everything done to avoid it, there comes a time when a broach starts. Twist in the mainsail now becomes useful rather than a bad thing. It is of little use just to ease the sheet, because one of two things usually happens. Either the backwind from the spinnaker prevents the sail freeing off enough, or else the boom drags in the water and has the same effect. The boat heels more, the rudder is ineffective as it is only partly immersed, and round she goes . . .

Thrust must be dumped from the mainsail before this situation occurs. Release the kicker and allow the boom to sky clear of the water, the wind escaping from the top of the sail and easing pressure. This demands instant action, so one man should be on the kicker and a second on the main sheet – the traveller has little effect under these conditions. Hydraulic vangs can be rather slow in their reaction to this sudden release, so some form of block and lever system is best. In addition keep as much weight as possible aft and to windward.

Releasing pressure from the spinnaker will reduce the tendency to bury the bow and also bring the boat more upright. As wind is now entering at the foot, letting the sheet run out will collapse the sail and quickly restore control, but of course it loses speed.

Light displacement craft with very short keels or dagger plates are so critical that they can broach going to windward, or at least on a very close reach. There is usually nothing which can be done to reduce heel by shifting more weight to windward – the crew should already be hanging on to the weather rail by their toenails. Similarly the Cunningham should be hard down to keep the mainsail draft forward. But bending the mast will flatten the sail and help considerably (or rake the whole rig forward if the rules allow).

Apart from the time lost, tip trucking or even a moderate broach can be highly dangerous in throwing people about the deck; if another boat is up to windward, the risk of collision is an additional problem. The winning crew will understand the forces involved and appreciate the interplay of the various controls available, so will be well placed to take steps before the situation gets out of hand.

6
Headsail Handling

There are those who say that an offshore racer should be able to be worked, including headsail changes, without disturbing the watch below, and there are those who say that the importance of maintaining maximum speed all the time demands the presence of all hands on deck for such operations.

It partly depends, of course, on the size of the boat and the strength of the crew. John Illingworth is on record in *Further Offshore* as advocating a large crew offshore, so that the watch below can rest in peace unless the boat encounters gale conditions; and there are those who turn out everyone even for a sail change, on the principle of doing it quickest with the mostest and relying on team spirit to maintain pressure even in the absence of sleep. The advent of the twin groove forestay has made headsail changing so much easier and quicker, that it should not normally be necessary to clutter the foredeck with too many bodies. You may find, however, that the boat you are on doesn't even work regular watches on relatively short races offshore. Much depends on the owner and the equipment, and there is not much you as a member of the crew can do except go along with the system. If life's too hectic at the sharp end, you don't have to go again, but don't ruin it for everyone else by grousing while you are there.

Choice of Sails

Later, when you have proved your worth, you may be called upon to contribute to the discussion on choice of which sails to put up in front of the mast; if so, put in your two cents' worth and then keep your counsel and accept the decision. The final choice will usually be made by the owner or skipper, and you will be expected right from the start to be able to produce the desired sail as it is called for; this is where your preparation earlier will pay off. In the case of headsails, you will be expected to know whether the watch master wants the whole thing, bag and all, on deck, or else just the tack passed up through the forehatch. If the decision is the latter, it follows that headsails should be stowed in their bags with the tack on top and the sail clear of tangles; very often the head and clew will be to hand as well. The use of sausage shaped bags with zipper or velcro fasteners will usually entail bringing it all on deck, in which case remember to lash the sailbag to a cleat or the life line before you pull out the sail, or you may suffer the ignominy of seeing it blown overboard as the sail comes free.

Bending Headsails

A headsail should be fastened at the tack first and then hanked to the forestay progressively from the lowest hank, unless it is going up in stops (figure 18) in which case the head is first made fast to the halyard and the sail slowly pulled up the stay and hanked on as it goes; the tack is then made fast last of all. Stops are normally only used on a headsail before the start of a race, when the helmsman wishes to change course rapidly without unduly tiring the crew with constant headsail sheeting. At the appropriate moment (usually around the five minute gun) the sail is cracked out and full power is available instantly. A headsail is sometimes also put up in stops during a sail change in heavy weather to stop it flogging unduly, or else at the end of a spinnaker run so that it is ready to break out as soon as the kite is taken down.

If a headfoil is used, the head of the genoa is led into the feeder and then into the groove with the halyard in place. See that the luff is flaked out (it should have been stowed in its bag with this in mind) so that it can run straight up without twists.

See that the sheets are properly rove, inside or outside the cap shrouds according to sail and point of sailing, also that the fairlead is correctly positioned. Only experience of the boat and sail concerned will tell you this and you must be guided by the watch master.

If a screw shackle is used to fasten the sail at the head, make sure that it is done up tight with a shackler, spike or pliers.

Changing Headsails

If the boat has one conventional forestay, clip the new headsail onto the wire below the bottom hank of the sail about to come down; you may need to undo the bottom hank to make room. Make sure that the new sail is rigged to leeward of the one it is replacing, because the old sail will then be inboard as it comes down. The old sail will have to come down first, but not until all is ready with the new one except tack and head. Fast down and fast up is the rule, and everyone should know what is expected of him.

The hand on the halyard should use his eyes to ensure that he doesn't lower away with such a rush that those who are gathering in the old sail are overwhelmed. The sheet can often be left cleated, except perhaps in the final stages of lowering, which will help stop the sail from flogging itself to death. The foredeck men should smother the sail quickly, using the technique explained already; it should then be tucked quickly under shockcord stretched across the deck, or otherwise held down, its hanks removed from the forestay, the halyard and sheet changed over and the new sail sent up. If you have to muzzle a headsail which is blowing away out of control, sit down on the deck and gather it in from this safe position.

With hanked headsails the boat has to be bald headed at some time during the change, unless you set a temporary inner staysail flying from the mast head to a point some five or six feet aft of the stem head. But good crew drill can cut down the time to less than a minute, so you will probably lose less ground by practising a slick change, than if you have three or more crewmen struggling and shouting on the foredeck; this will louse up the slot for the three or four minutes it takes to set an inner staysail, lower the old headsail, hoist and trim the replacement and then lower and stow the temporary staysail.

The arrival of the twin groove headfoil has changed the scene somewhat. A replacement genoa can be set and trimmed by three hands before the same men then take in the old one. If a second winch is not available, lock off the old sheet on a jammer to free the winch, bend a second sheet to the clew of the new sail, hoist it to leeward of the old one and trim roughly to the same camber. The old sail can then be taken down by the two men forward while the cockpit hand fine-tunes the new sail. The slightly awkward problem

81

of hoisting to leeward of the old sail can be overcome if the change is made as the boat is about to be tacked. Hoist the new sail to windward, tack, then take down the old sail also now to windward. If you have neither a second winch nor a sheet jammer, you probably won't have a twin groove headfoil, but if you do, the switch can still be made, either by tacking as just described, or else by sheeting the new sail direct to a cleat and then changing to the winch as the old sail is released; it's a bit of a struggle but it can be done.

If you are running before the wind, be careful not to hoist the new sail so tightly that you take the strain on the luff of the sail rather than the forestay; the mast will be pushed forward by the mainsail, thus taking the weight off the forestay, and it is easy to set up a situation where the headsail is overstrained as soon as the boat comes on the wind again and the mast is pulled back. Look at the halyard marks if these are on the mast, and check with the watch master that you have the correct limit in mind.

Practice

It is at night that headsails can waste time. A well drilled crew can save several minutes if they know their job, have practised assiduously and are left to get on with it. It is important to settle beforehand exactly what each man is to do, particularly in heavy weather when passing orders on deck may be made difficult by the noise of the wind and water. Under these circumstances too, the skipper should always try to give his crew enough warning of a headsail change for them to get into wet weather gear. You will not need to be told that there is a natural reluctance to get soaked, but you may need reminding that it is only by getting right up to the sharp end – in both senses of the phrase – that the job will be done quickly. It is, therefore, worth repeating here for the sake of those owners and skippers who may be still with us, that a dry crewman, properly protected against the elements, is more likely to get stuck into the job than a pyjama-clad zombie pushed onto the foredeck as a reluctant sacrifice, simply because the skipper couldn't think ahead or is impatient.

A sail change, then, is usually undertaken after some debate and should not normally be a panic measure, although there are of course exceptions which warrant exceptional measures. If you hear such a debate going on and it looks a bit wet up front, get ready without waiting to be told. Too many sail changes at short notice will betray indecision and will undermine morale, even if they do not sap the energy of the watch below to the point where they lose efficiency and keenness when it comes to their turn on deck.

Bowsprits

If you are unlucky enough to ship in an old fashioned cutter with a bowsprit, be prepared for a wet trip. Apart from any other consideration, you should quite seriously take double the change of clothing you would otherwise pack. Sooner or later somebody will have to go out to the end of the bowsprit to change the jib. Even if it is normally pulled out on the end of a traveller (unlikely on an offshore racer of any mettle, due to the difficulty of ensuring a tight luff), the time will come when the system jams and needs sorting out on site. Don't volunteer for this job if you are uncertain of your footing on a bobstay, or your mother thinks you are liable to go down with one of your chesty colds if you get damp. This is the occasion when you should have one, if not two, hands for yourself and one for the boat. She will be unbalanced weightwise, because there will almost certainly be somebody else on the foredeck to watch the fun, and so much weight forward will add to any tendency to bury her nose. Hook on, be prepared for repeated duckings, breathe only when the bow comes up, and come back if it becomes too much for you (you will only be a liability frozen into a petrified figurehead half way between safety and the place where action is needed). Owners of bowsprit cutters should seriously consider having a wet suit as part of the boat's permanent gear.

Light Weather

I now wish to examine the factors behind headsail drill under various conditions; we will take light weather work to windward to start with. The single most important hint for a novice crewman in light weather is not to leap about the place. The helmsman will be trying his best to concentrate on the job in hand and won't want to be disturbed. In addition, and just as important, the balance of the boat should not be upset.

If a headsail has to be changed, wait for orders before you rush forward. The presence of men on the foredeck will seriously alter the trim of the boat and reduce her speed. If you are, in fact, needed up front, there is a way of walking which must be learned and which won't jar the boat or jog the wind out of her sails. It entails creeping surefooted with slightly bent knees in a kind of gliding motion, taking care to place the feet on deck rather than stepping. Tread softly, do the job and get back to your station without unnecessary delay.

Trim

Sail trimming is always important, but in light weather it assumes greater significance. This is because the boat will be sailing below her maximum speed the entire time, so any improvement in thrust will be of continuing benefit; in heavy weather you may be going at full speed for most of the time, so the finer points are wasted except in the lulls. It is important to examine critically the flow in all sails at regular intervals, and you will be expected to contribute your comments if you spot something which can be improved. I am not asking you to be a perpetual critic, for ever coming up with suggestions for altering the trim of a well balanced sail plan. If the boat is going well, there is a lot to be said in light winds for remaining absolutely quiet while the helmsman gets on with the job of working to windward. You will easily get a reputation for never letting well alone if you are constantly offering unsolicited criticism. Nevertheless, regular inspection of sail trim is an important part of driving a racing yacht offshore, and the sheet will almost certainly be left uncleated with one man trimming to wind changes: harden slightly in puffs and ease again as it slackens.

'How's the genny?'

This probably means that the owner or helmsman feels that the boat is not properly in the groove. If you are sail trimming, don't just grunt a pacifying word of encouragement; take a walk forward and have a look at the sail from in front, look aloft, check mast bend and flow in both main and genoa, examine the slot, look to the leeches and then pronounce judgement.

Luff Tension

In accordance with the theory we have discussed, you may be called upon to ease the headsail halyard or tack downhaul (Cunningham hole). If this is the case, get to the rope or line in question, look to whoever will call the trim be it helmsman, skipper, owner, watch master or specialist sail trimmer, and call clearly.

'Easing away now.'

You should then ease steadily and positively for several inches, pause if you think you have let enough go and have not been told to stop and, so that the sail trimmer shall know that you are not still easing, call again.

'How's that?'

The object is to ensure that whoever is calling the trim shall not be in any doubt as to whether you are still easing away; you are not trying to fool him. He may well need to go forward and examine the luff of the sail from the pulpit – almost certainly he will have to do this at night, with the aid of a flashlight.

Sheets

As I said earlier, a headsail is more sensitive to adjustment of the sheet than a mainsail. This is because altering the sheet also alters the camber; in addition, the main driving force of the sailplan comes from the headsail. As with luff tension, you should look to the sail trimmer for your instructions and there should be only one person delegated to this task. Don't cleat up too soon, but wait until the trimmer has had a chance to assess all the factors. It follows that you should not interfere if someone else is easing the sheet, unless you have been specifically asked to go forward and check the flow. In this case remember the shape we examined in the chapter on theory, and try to see that the result conforms: a nice curve to the front half of the sail and a flat leech. Too tight a sheet will show along the foot of the sail, which will bear against the bottom of the cap shroud; the upper leech may also press against the spreader end.

Fairlead

More flow can be given to the lower half of a headsail, on the wind in the light conditions we are considering, by letting the fairlead go forward, but care should be taken not to overdo it or the leech will go hard. Equally it may be advantageous to switch to a more in-

85

board lead if the water is smooth, as the boat will then point higher; the precaution here is not to point so high that the speed drops off.

Leechline

If the leech drums badly going to windward, you may be asked to correct it by judicious use of the leechline. You should pull in just enough to steady the vibration, but not so much that the leech curls and backwinds the mainsail. You are trying to stop the sail shaking so that the whole of the airflow pattern round the combined headsail/mainsail aerofoil is disturbed; you will at the same time remove an irritating noise which can undermine the concentration of the helmsman. Your presence in the slot will itself do a lot of harm to the flow pattern, so don't hang about admiring the scenery, but do the job quickly and get back to your station. If there is no cleat or button on the sail, be sure to tie the cord with a knot which will not slip, but which can be undone quickly again when the time is ripe; try a rolling hitch.

Light Weather Headsails

If the skipper orders a light weather headsail in conditions of under force 2, it is worth asking if he wants it hanked to the forestay or not. Under close reaching conditions, where the spinnaker will be too shy, it sometimes pays to set the ghoster flying. This makes it a quicker and easier job to replace it with a heavier genoa if the wind pipes up, because the new sail can be hanked on and hoisted before the ghoster is taken down. Indeed, it makes a change mandatory if the skipper wants to keep a straight luff, and he thus avoids the common error of holding on too long to a light headsail in a freshening breeze, thus stretching it out of shape.

Kedging

While we are on the subject of light weather, we can have a look at the tactical side of kedging. There are two occasions when you can speak up, even as a new man. The first is to check the boat's speed over the ground in ghosting conditions. If you are in sight of land or a mark of any kind, try to establish a transit or range – two objects in line – so that you can tell how you are doing. You may be slipping through the water yet still going backwards over the ground due to the tide or current, so an early kedge would enable you to stay still and let your rivals drop back round you. Concentration on getting the boat to sail at her best may have made everyone forget to notice this little fact, so you should move quietly towards the watch master and then get him to check for himself.

Your second contribution could be to suggest kedging over the stern under certain circumstances. If you are drifting towards the starting line with five minutes to go and it is obvious that you are going to have to kedge to avoid being over at the start, or if you are coming up to a turning mark on the tide and can see that some of your rivals ahead have kedged to stop themselves being carried too far beyond it, it pays to stop short of the line or mark still pointing the way you want to go; so put the kedge over the stern. You will then be ready to move off when the gun goes or the wind gets up, without having to turn round first with little or no steerage way on; see figures 28 and 29. One point, don't forget that he who kedges first has right of way over those who do so later.

Heavy Weather

Weather heavy enough to cause you to change down from a full sized genoa to a No. 2 or smaller will, quite possibly, mean a reef sooner or later. This will bring you onto the foredeck without worrying about considerations of fore and aft trim. It will also get you wet, so see that you are dressed for the job; see also that you obey the ship's ruling on harnesses. We have already discussed ways and means of changing headsails, and it is only my intention here to talk about the whys and wherefores.

There will be a lot of wind trying to get through the slot, and a full sized genoa without much hollow to the leech will make it hard for this to happen without blockage occurring. This will build up turbulence and destroy the smooth airflow, which will be evidenced by a heavily backwinded mainsail. A No. 2 genoa will have a shorter foot, cut high so that it doesn't pick up a lot of water as the boat heels, and it will almost certainly have a hollow leech; all this will improve the airflow. More important from your point of view, it may need alteration to the fore and aft position of the fairlead and you should be ready to remind the watch leader of this if he forgets; the fairlead will certainly have to be as far outboard as possible if there is a choice. Look critically at the leech for signs of a hook or curl.

Beating to windward in strong winds demands a sail as flat as you can get it, so you should not be afraid to put your weight both on the halyard and the sheet winches when the time comes. Make sure that the handle is properly in the winch while cranking and stow it carefully after you have finished.

Reaching

An offshore racer will normally reach with only a genoa (i.e. without a spinnaker) in wild weather or when the wind is well forward of the beam; even then, modern reaching spinnakers (gennikers, spankers, star-cut spinnakers and the like) are narrowing the relative wind angle at which these sails can be carried successfully. We shall see later, in the chapter on spinnakers, how a big 'chute can slow the boat considerably when the wind is well forward of the beam, due to its pressing effect when it is strapped alongside, and we have already discussed how it is a major factor in causing a broach. We shall consider separately the question of using headsails with the spinnaker, but I want now to look briefly at the mainsail and genoa situation on the reach.

If in this section I refer largely to headsails it is not only because this chapter is devoted to these sails, but also because they react well to proper trim. Don't forget the mainsail, however, for careful attention to clew outhaul, slider and sheet will repay the effort.

Light Weather

In very light reaching conditions the sheet will weigh too heavily on the genoa and it may pay to switch to a lighter line; this may be a single sheet tied to the clew (with a bowline) to save the additional weight of a shackle. It becomes everybody's responsibility to remember to fit a second sheet if the boat comes on the wind and may have to tack. The fairlead should be right outboard and can sometimes be taken aft to help ease the slot by allowing a little more twist to the sail.

Leechline

When broad reaching in light weather, the leechline may be tightened with advantage. This gives the aft part of the headsail more of a bag and there is little danger of upsetting the airflow in the lee of the mainsail at the slow wind speeds we are considering. Here again, however, it is important to remember the special conditions prevailing and that it has to be slackened again if they change, for instance if you come on the wind.

Sheets

The sheets will probably not be cleated, but each given over to one crewman to play. If you are assigned this task, give it your undivided attention, for you can quite literally double the boat's average speed in light airs. Either play it directly to the fairlead or, if the wind is more than five or six knots, put one or more turns on the winch and play it from there. You should be constantly easing the sheet until the luff starts to lift, and then hardening it so that the sail is full. Remember that a boat going to windward would experience constant minor wind shifts and would have to luff and bear away all the time. You want the sail to drive as much forward with as little sideways pull as possible, so you should be for ever seeking to take advantage of any free puffs. Some crews do this assiduously with the genoa but forget the mainsail; it is a painstaking job which will well reward steady application and I cannot recommend it too highly.

Heavy Weather

Reaching under headsails in wild weather imposes the problem of sail trimming when the forces involved are heavy. It is tempting to think that the boat is moving at her maximum speed so that the finer points are wasted, and this is often the case. But do not allow yourself to be lured into a lazy attitude, because there are always lulls in the wind, and also the possibility of picking up a few extra knots in surfing down the back of a wave from time to time; crews in very light displacement boats have to pay constant attention to trim if they want to stay on the plane. It will take two of you to tend the headsail sheet if you do not have self-tailing winches, one to tail and one to crank the handle, but give it plenty of attention.

In chapter five we discussed the reasons and cures for broaching. If the boat you are in has a tendency towards this distressing habit, the skipper may ease the mainsail a bit and push her along on the headsail. Correct trim becomes important on such occasions and it is one of the few circumstances when an overtrimmed headsail may be recommended (it will help to hold her head off the wind). If you are put on the kicking strap or boom vang, be sure that you keep your wits about you, because you have to respond instantly to any shout to let the boom go skyward in order to dump wind from the main. If she does broach badly, the best advice is to hold on tight and wait for her to come up again – which she ought to do in her own time as the wind comes out of the sails. Keep your eyes open to what is happening around you, and be ready to lend a hand if anyone starts to go overboard. Don't forget my advice about getting weight aft in the boat.

Headsails with the Spinnaker

Use of a headsail with the spinnaker will be decided for you by the skipper. The factors he will have to consider are disturbance of the spinnaker, the drive contributed directly by the headsail, and the improvement to the airflow which modern headsails like the tallboy or slat sail can bring.

As far as you are concerned, my previous warning against crowding unnecessarily onto the foredeck, thereby pushing the bow down, still holds good. Wait until you are ordered forward before rushing into the fray. If you have to go, do your job and get back quickly.

A full sized reacher seems to set best under the 'chute with the wind just forward or just abaft the beam. It is a big sail with a high clew, which can disturb the airflow across the spinnaker, so the spinnaker pole should be topped up slightly to carry the tack as far forward of the luff of the reacher as possible (the pole at right angles to the forestay will do this). If the two sails continue to interfere with each other, it is a sign that the boat would be happier with a shorter hoist sail such as a conventional spinnaker staysail, or with the reacher pulled down to a second tack eye six feet or so up the luff. Such is the effectiveness of good sail trimming, however, that many boats set a staysail tacked some way aft of the stem as well as a genoa under the spinnaker when the conditions are right. If the three sails are not to louse up the airflow completely, this calls for careful siting of the staysail tack and fairlead, together with some delicate trimming of all the sheets.

The Tallboy

The tallboy or slat sail is a tall, slim sail with a very short foot, which is set in front of the mainsail off the wind in order to clean up the airflow to leeward. By acting in the same way as the slat of an aircraft's wing, it cuts down turbulence, increases the local speed of airflow and thus improves thrust; see figure 16. It is a difficult sail to set properly and much depends on the position of the tack and the sheet fairlead. The former can be nearly on the centreline or right out on the weather rail; the latter can trim the sail almost athwartships (on the run) or nearer to the fore and aft line (for a close reach). The basic object is to use the tallboy to extend the area of the mainsail beyond its luff, with the tallboy leech close to the lee side of the mainsail, so that it reintroduces the venturi which has been opened up too much now that the leech of the genoa has either been eased away on the reach or removed altogether under spinnaker; the tallboy tack will thus normally be somewhere in line with the main boom on the forward side of the mast, while its clew will be sheeted fairly close to the lee side of the mainsail. To achieve this infinite variety, some boats use a system of adjustable strut which can be operated from the cockpit, while others depend on wire strops or rails. Be ready to tack or sheet anywhere on the foredeck and don't argue if the position seems outlandish – they know their boat and you don't, however much of a theorist you may be. At all events, the long legs of an offshore race make it worth while to spend a little time setting up the tallboy accurately, whereas a boat may lose more ground than she gains on a day race inshore; the debating society meeting on the foredeck to adjust tack and clew will slow the boat more than the final result can retrieve, even though the sail sets perfectly, before the boat has to come on the wind again when sailing short legs. This is a sail which is not much used these days.

If you are required to make fast the tack of a spinnaker staysail or tallboy by means of a length of line to a specific point on deck

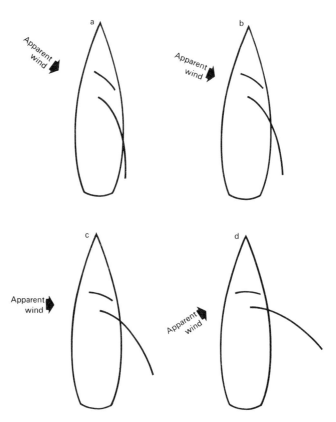

16 The tallboy The tallboy or slat sail forms the slot at the leading edge of the mainsail again, when the genoa is either eased so that the venturi between the mainsail and genoa is lessened, or the headsail is removed altogether in favour of a spinnaker. The tallboy should lie just forward of the luff of the mainsail and parallel with it, so that the wind may pass easily between them and be smoothed out. It follows that both tack and clew positions must be infinitely variable, the former coming aft and outboard as the wind comes aft, while the latter goes outboard and forward.

(possibly a deadeye or the weather pulpit rail), besides the exact location of the tack point, find out how long a tack pendant to allow (and thus how high above deck the sail will be). You may be presented with six feet of line and the skipper may want the sail hard down on the deck or close to the pulpit rail out of the way of the spinnaker's airflow, or he may prefer it with a foot or so of slack to get the sail up a bit into cleaner air free of the deck. If you have to set the sail up a bit, try to get a line long enough to allow you to have a double or treble part to and from the tack; finish off with a rolling hitch or possibly a Tarbuck knot (see chapter 9).

The Bigboy

The bigboy or blooper is set opposite the spinnaker when the wind is force 3 or more and is within 30 degrees of dead aft. It has been said that the sail merely serves to make the helmsman blind ahead, but adds little to boat speed; that it owes its popularity to crews who find it easy to set and satisfying in the impression it gives of extra area grabbing otherwise unused wind. But this takes no account of the steadying effect of the sail in conditions of rhythmic rolling. I'm not saying that it prevents rolling, but it certainly delays the onset. As soon as the wind comes more than 30 degrees from dead aft, however, the sail should be handed and replaced by the genoa and/or a staysail; it is also of no use in less than seven or eight knots of wind, as it tends to hang lifeless from its rather slack halyard.

The main danger is that the crew will get over-interested in trimming 'their' sail and will forget the spinnaker.

'If you ease the pole a bit,' they cry, 'the bigboy will set better.'

This can so easily mean loss of thrust from the sail which really is big, in order to get a marginal improvement from the blooper. Be warned.

Stowing Headsails

Stopping

Hanked headsails are sometimes set up in stops to aid control of the sail and to save time and energy. To stop a headsail, the head should be made fast and as much of the luff as possible pulled out straight with the leech pulled out alongside it. The sail is then gathered from the middle towards the luff and leech, making sure that the leech is on the outside of the roll or bunch, next to the luffwire or luffrope at the finish. If stopping cotton or yarn is used, place the stops next to the hanks so that there will be a firm attachment to pull against when they are broken out. One turn only is placed round the sail next to each of the upper hanks (if the top hank is within six feet of the head, leave this without a stop in light weather as, without much wind, it may not break out easily). Gradually increase the number of turns towards the foot and put half a dozen each side of the clew (which should, of course, protrude so that the sheets may be bent on), where there is plenty of power to break out the sail. On a low cut sail like a genoa, the clew will be very near to the tack if the leech has been pulled down properly; a working jib clew will be higher and there will probably be two or three stops below it. It is important to see that the luff is

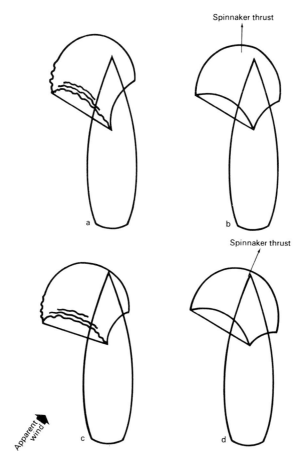

17 *Spinnaker sheet adjustment* The object of spinnaker sheet adjustment is to get the sail pulling forwards and not sideways. If the sheet is eased too much, as in (a), the luff will fall in and the whole sail will collapse if not corrected. Proper trim on a broad reach should enable the whole sail to pull directly forward as in (b), but if, with the sheet trimmed correctly, the pole is then squared too far aft, the sail will collapse again as in (c). The most common fault in spinnaker sheet trim is to sheet the sail too hard as in (d); even though the pole is correctly square to the wind, the drive of the sail is partly sideways so loss of speed must result. You can often tell that this is happening because the foot of the spinnaker starts to bear on the forestay; if you can't ease the sheet and keep the sail full, the pole is probably too far aft and must also go forward.

pulled straight and tight during the stopping process, or the stops will break out accidentally as they are strained when the luffrope or wire tightens on the forestay as the sail is hoisted.

You may find that the boat you are aboard uses rubber bands for stopping sails. In this case a band is looped over each hank, the two parts are passed round the sail and the other end of the band is looped over the hank from the other direction; see figure 18.

Bagging

It is important to good sail drill that headsails should be bagged properly. If you have hanked sails, it will usually be the practice to put the sails untwisted into conventional bags, with the head, tack and clew on top ready to receive their respective attachments. Groove luff headsails are nearly always stowed these days in sausage shaped bags, with the luff carefully flaked on top of the stow and the three corners readily to hand. If you have not previously done this, it is quickly learned by watching the process once.

Synthetic cloth creases readily, but big sails are not easy to fold on board. The sail most affected by creases will be the light genoa. It will probably be made from canvas somewhere between 3–5 ounces, which is easily creased and which will not have enough wind in it to blow it flat; like a spinnaker, a ghoster of 1–2 ounce material will not crease badly, and the heavier cloth of a No 1 genoa will resist creases to a certain extent and these will tend to disappear above force 3. So try always to fold and roll any headsail made from light canvas, so that haphazard creases are kept to a minimum and particularly away from the vulnerable leech area.

7
Spinnaker Handling

Spinnakers have had such a lot written about them that you would be forgiven for thinking that they are not worth all this bother if they are so difficult. On the contrary, however, it is precisely because they are such racewinners that people take such trouble to discuss them and skippers to understand and tame them.

One of the companion volumes in this series, *Sail Racer* by Jack Knights, has something to say about the spinnaker and I have written a bit about it myself in *Sails*, so I do not need to delve too closely into detail here. Different boats use different systems of setting, gybing and handing the spinnaker, dictated by owner's or skipper's preference, size of boat, rigging layout or, possibly, by lack of research into the subject. As a new member of an established team, you will have to fall into line and adapt to the routine which has evolved on board: one or two pole gybe, internal outhaul, hoist from a turtle or in stops, single or double ended poles and so on, the variations are many. Here we shall deal with your immediate problems as a foredeck or cockpit hand, what background you need to know, how you must react and why. Leave the planning and devising to others, but be ready for anything they may cook up. I apologise for any duplication which follows, or indeed any difference of opinion with the pundits, but the one is important for recapitulation and the other shows variety.

To start with you probably already know that, for most of its life, a spinnaker has the wind flowing across it from luff to leech; the exception is when the wind is within a ten degree arc of dead astern, at which time it blows into the middle and out at each side (and the bottom). It follows that it nearly always acts like a giant headsail and should be considered as such. It has two drawbacks and two advantages on the headsail.

The luff of a spinnaker can never be as taut and as straight as that of a headsail. Similarly, the leech is bellied so that it does not have a flat run off to the wind like a headsail.

On the other hand, a spinnaker not only has an adjustable clew like a headsail, it also has an adjustable tack. Secondly, the spinnaker is larger than any headsail which the boat can carry, and that's what it's all about: more area, more power.

Your task as a crewman will be to get that power switched on and off quickly without fuss and so to control it that it is acting to best advantage all the time. To do this you must understand what the drawbacks and advantages of the spinnaker mean in practical terms; you must be surefooted and, at times, strong; you must fit into the teamwork with a sound knowledge of what is expected of you; and you must develop your observation and judgement so that you can contribute plus values to the team.

Hoisting

In marginal spinnaker conditions your immediate object should be to show your skipper that you have enough knowledge and judgement to be asked your opinion on whether the boat would go better with the 'chute up. In your early days you are more likely to be asked to assess the relative wind strength and angle on the next leg of the course from the available evidence, while opinions on actually carrying the sail will be sought elsewhere. Once you have contributed your bit, keep your mouth shut and wait for the decision. Matters are now out of your hands and the skipper must be left in peace to consider the evidence and give his verdict – he will ask again if he wants any more information.

As soon as the spinnaker is ordered on deck, get on with the job you have been allocated and get on with it quickly. Speed is almost always important when hoisting and lowering the kite, because its power is such that you want it as soon as possible and you want to keep it going as long as you can. I don't mean to imply that you should rush about the place reeving lines, humping the spinnaker in its turtle or clipping on sheets and guys in a frenzy of effort. You will not only get in everybody's way but your restlessness will distract the helmsman at a critical period and, in light winds, your very energy will upset the balance of the boat. What is required now is a smooth controlled co-ordination, so that each member of the crew does precisely what is expected of him and doesn't interfere with his colleagues who are doing precisely what is expected of them. If your job is in the cockpit and you see a guy come unclipped on the pulpit, don't rush forward to add to the scrum on the foredeck, call out to the watch master. He will get it snapped on again in less time than he will take to find out what the hell you think you are doing suddenly appearing at his elbow, when he thought you were ready to take in the sheet back aft.

The first obvious difference you will notice in spinnaker drill from one boat to another is how it is hoisted. Most yachts use some form of turtle, or patent bag, to contain the sail conveniently so that it is ready to slip on and be hoisted direct from the turtle, which is fixed conveniently for the process. Some of the bigger boats, however, hoist their spinnakers in stops in everything but light weather.

The Turtle

The basic object of a spinnaker turtle is to have the sail in a special bag so that the head and clews are sticking out ready for their appropriate lines. The spinnaker can then be hoisted straight into action. It follows that the sail must be untwisted when it is stowed in the turtle, with its three corners put in last. In practice, a spinnaker is bagged by hooking the head to a point in the cabin. Each leech is then traced along its length to see that it is free from twists and it is flaked back and forth into one hand as you go. The main bunt of the sail is then thrust into the turtle, preferably with the foot going first into the bottom, although this is not essential. Finally, the leeches are pushed in last with the head and clews carefully protruding from the middle and either side respectively. The turtle usually has some form of quick release fastening so that the sail is firmly contained until it is wanted, but which will open automatically as the halyard pulls the head from the bag: elastic, Velcro grip fastening or quick release buttons.

Stopping

A spinnaker is stopped in a similar manner to a headsail. The head is made fast, the two stays (or luffs or leeches whichever you prefer to call them) are pulled taut side by side, the bunt of the sail is gathered (not rolled) towards the stays and stopping cotton is tied round at 3–6 foot intervals, depending on the size of the sail; once

98

again, don't put a stop too near the head, particularly in light weather.

Spinnakers can, however, more quickly be stopped by using rubber bands and a length of plastic piping or, on larger sails, a plastic bucket with the bottom removed. The diameter of the tube should be one inch for every 8–10 feet of height of spinnaker or 'I' measurement. If you meet this system, you merely slip sufficient bands onto the piping or bucket before you start (one band for every 3–6 feet of sail, depending on size), feed the spinnaker into the mouth of the bucket, making sure that the luff and leech are pulled

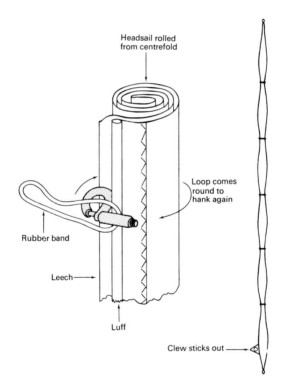

18 *Stopping headsails with rubber bands* The sail is pulled out so that luff and leech are stretched straight side by side; the rest of the sail is then bunched or rolled to join these two. One end of the loop of a rubber band is passed over each piston hank, the rest of the band is taken round the back of the sail and the other loop passed over the same hank from the other direction. Take care that both luff and leech are properly pulled out, or the bands will be subjected to excessive stretch as the sail tries to ride up or down the luff in order to equalise itself as the luff is pulled straight on hoisting.

out side by side, and slip a band off at the appropriate intervals as it is passed through. The sail is now stopped.

As with headsails, it is important to see that the spinnaker is pulled out taut during this operation, for the stops may break out as the sail goes up if it is unevenly gathered with one stay bunched against its fellow. If the watch master considers that the wind is not going to be strong enough to break the sail out right up to the head, you may be required to break the topmost stop by hand as the sail is actually hoisted. If the top stop is stubborn after the sail is up, you will waste a good deal of time heaving on the leech trying to snap it and this will not only delay full development of power, it will rock wind out of all the sails and slow the boat right down.

Usually the boat will reach the turning mark, bear away onto a run, and the spinnaker will be hoisted to leeward of the genoa. All must be ready for instant action so that not a second is lost in getting the sail up, the pole aft and the sail drawing by trimming the sheet. Where the boat has to gybe or tack at the mark, valuable seconds can be gained by hoisting the spinnaker in stops to wind-ward of the genoa while still close hauled. There is, of course, a danger here of the sail breaking out of its stops inadvertently while it is flogging about in the slot for the last seconds of the beat; if this happens you will lose all and more that you were trying to gain. If the procedure succeeds, however, the sail is up and ready to crack out as soon as the boat is on the other gybe or tack. Care must be taken to see that the tack of the sail and the guy are correctly rove to windward round the forestay before the tack or gybe is made, or chaos will result.

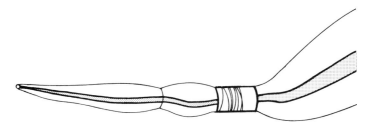

19 *Stopping a spinnaker with rubber bands* Pull both luffs (or leeches) out side by side and feed the sail through some sort of tube onto which has been placed a series of rubber bands. The diameter of the tube should be 1 in. for every 8–10 ft of sail luff, which means a plastic bucket with the bottom carefully removed for a 50 ft boat, or a piece of plastic drainpipe for a 30 footer. Slip a band off the tube at intervals of about 4–6 ft as the sail is pulled through, and it is then stopped.

Practice

All this drama goes on with you as a small cog in the middle but, just like any set of gears, the small cog can still bring it to a grinding halt if it gets out of mesh. You must know your job and, just as important, you must practise it. If you are frightened to fly the kite, you will surely lose it when you do finally pluck up your courage. Don't let it be the master, and the best way of dominating the thing is to put it up, gybe it, fly it shy, gybe it again, lower it and then put it up again. Do it until you can nearly do it blindfolded.

This advice, however, won't help you if you don't have the chance to carry it out before the race, or if you join a well-drilled crew as the extra man. They know already how to do it and your object is not to let them down. First and foremost, therefore, don't pretend to knowledge which you do not possess; the sail will soon find you out. Rather should you minimise your experience until you know how your own ability fits into the rest of the crew. The beginner should wait for orders and do what he is told. Obvious pitfalls to be avoided are failure to make the sailbag fast if the spinnaker is hoisted out of it; reeving sheet or guy wrongly (outside everything is all very well, but there are exceptions – the foreguy, for instance, often comes aft through the lifeline); snapping on sheet, guy or halyard without checking that they are clear; pulling or letting go the wrong line; not attending to the free end of a halyard (ever watched the tail of a halyard snake its way to freedom aloft?). If in doubt, check and double check, even if it costs you a few more seconds and a roasting from the watch master.

Trim

The object of spinnaker trim, as with other sails, is to adjust the set of the sail so as to produce the maximum forward thrust. It is easier to see the effect of trim on a spinnaker than it is on fore and aft sails, partly because the sail is more obviously pulling the boat along and partly because it collapses more completely than a mainsail or jib which is allowed to free off a little too far.

There is only room in this chapter to deal with the basic rules of spinnaker trim; if you want them, the finer points are dealt with in *Sails*. In any case, you won't be calling the shots at this stage of your offshore racing career, so you can learn as you go along. We must start with first principles so that you know what you are trying to achieve.

Spinnaker Pole

The further away from the mast the tack of the spinnaker can be trimmed, the wider the spread of the sail to catch the wind. The more at right angles to the wind direction the pole is, the further across the wind flow will be the tack and so, once again, the more wind will be collected. The former demands a spinnaker pole at right angles to the mast in the horizontal plane; the latter requires that the pole shall always be at right angles to the wind direction. There are exceptions, but don't let's get involved with them at this point.

Spinnaker Clews

The tack and clew of a spinnaker should normally be the same height above water. This ensures that the sail is not twisted, which would give an oblique thrust.

Spinnaker Sheet

Once the pole angle and tack height have been set, the sheet should usually be eased until the luff of the sail *just* starts to collapse, where-upon it should be hardened slightly so that the sail is completely full. This ensures that the spinnaker is so angled that its thrust is directed as far forward as possible.

Reaching

When reaching under spinnaker there is often a tendency to hang onto the sail when the wind comes too far ahead. The boat is heeling over, throwing a certain amount of white water about and seems to be thrashing along well. Under these circumstances it is sometimes salutory to divide the spinnaker mentally in two down the middle. The front half will be doing its job of adding to thrust all right, but have a good look at the rear half. You may well find that it is only contributing to the heel forces and even actually trying to pull you backwards. The skipper has to decide whether a genoa would pull you along better and this will largely depend on the relative sizes of the two sails and on the wind strength. In medium winds (force 3–4) a working spinnaker can usually be carried to advantage with the wind 5 degrees forward of the beam for every amount by which it exceeds the size of the largest jib which would replace it. Most IOR spinnakers are two and a half to three times the size of the associated genoa, so the former pays up to 75 degrees wind angle. This angle varies with wind strength and flatness of the spinnaker. As I said in chapter five, if the boat broaches readily it often pays to use a double headsail rig when the wind is forward of the beam.

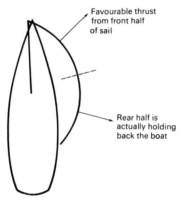

Favourable thrust
from front half
of sail

Rear half is
actually holding
back the boat

20 *Spinnaker on a close reach* A spinnaker which is either too full or else sheeted too far forward on a close reach will have a bellied leech. The area gain over the genoa will be lost through the after part of the spinnaker producing a rearward element of thrust as well as heeling the boat a lot. The front half has to overcome this drag before it contributes to pulling the boat along; a decent genoa would often do better.

Chafe

Chafe is sufficiently important to have a heading and a paragraph of its own. Spinnaker nylon is, as you will know, a lightweight material. It is thus subject to chafe more than fore and aft sails, so should be especially protected from its effects by trimming appropriately. The most likely point of attack is where the spinnaker foot bears against the forestay, if the sheet is too tight or the pole too far aft on a reach. You share with everyone on board a responsibility to guard against this danger at all times, but particularly at night, or the first you will know will be a tearing rip which will bring all hands on deck at the double. Even if the foot tape itself is only

103

lightly rubbing on the forestay, don't shrug it off as of little account due to its minor nature. An hour or so will soon see the sail in ribbons, even in light winds. Watch out also for chafe on sheets and guys, particularly where they run under the main boom or across the guardwires; they can often be led through snatch blocks shackled to the boom end or a jockey pole can be rigged to keep them clear.

Gybing

Spinnakers are at their most interesting during the gybe. Do it right and you gain ground; snarl it up and you drop out of the reckoning. Practice makes perfect and you should take every opportunity to swing that sail from side to side. There are so many variations on the single pole or twin pole gybe (even those which require nobody on the foredeck at all) that I won't confuse you with too many diagrams and explanations. It is worth looking superficially at some of the commoner systems, however, to know enough about their basic principles to assess their relative advantages and disadvantages.

To achieve one or other of these systems of gybe, certain gear is required and we should know the options.

Sheets/Guys

It is simplest to have one rope attached to each lower corner, or clew, of the spinnaker, so that they take it in turns to be sheet and guy according to which gybe the boat is on. Rope is easy to handle and cleat and, with coloured warps, there can be no confusion about which line is doing which job. As the size of the spinnaker increases, however, the loadings in the sail and on the lines reach a point where stretch on the guy becomes excessive; a certain amount of give in the sheet can be tolerated, but the guy should anchor the spinnaker pole firmly without allowing it to wander back and forth at the whim of the wind. Unless no-stretch rope is used, therefore, we find wire guys becoming necessary; in practice this can be related to boats of about 40 feet overall length. These craft still need rope sheets, however, for ease of handling, so their spinnakers have a wire guy and a rope sheet on each clew, one of each being a lazy sheet or guy on each gybe.

104

Single or Twin Poles

The other basic difference about spinnaker systems is the question of single or twin pole gybing. The single pole method is simplest, as less gear is involved, but here again size of boat affects the issue. The basic principle is that the single pole system allows the spinnaker to float free while the pole is dipped through the foretriangle, with the attendant danger that it will collapse due to lack of control. The twin pole method ensures that there is always one pole hard up against a clew at all times, because the new pole is set right up and the spinnaker drawn down to its end before the old pole is released (so for a short period during the actual gybe the sail has a pole on each clew – or tack, whichever you prefer to call it); this means that the spinnaker is completely under firm control at all times. The twin pole method demands twin sheets and guys, be they rope or wire, because the complete system has to be rove on the new pole ready to take over on the new windward side, while a new sheet must also be available to take over its duties by taking the strain off the old guy at the appropriate moment, so that the 'dead' pole can be released and stowed. A single pole system can be used with either single or twin sheets and guys, but a twin pole system cannot be used with single sheets and guys.

Mast Fitting

Poles will usually fix into a cup on a slider on the forward side of the mast; the pole locks automatically as its end is pushed into the cup. In some cases this means that only one end of the pole will fit the cup, because the fitting for attaching to the guy or sail is too cumbersome to go into the mast socket; this means that you have what is known as a single ended pole. It is better to have both ends capable of going into the cup and of fastening to the guy or sail – a so-called double ended pole. Small boats usually have poles which fasten to a ring on the mast slider by means of a piston plunger. Be it cup or ring, the mast fitting should be capable of adjustment up and down on a slide; large boats will have a rope tackle or mechanical device for this adjustment.

Piston Plunger End

This works much like an end pull piston hank and is usually operated by means of a line stretched along the length of the spinnaker pole. It can either clip direct onto a ring on the clew of the sail or, more usually, onto the guy. Its advantages are that it is operated positively by hand pull on the line, its mechanism is simple – with attendant good serviceability – and the same fitting can go at each end of the pole because it can also attach to a ring on the mast or fit into a cup. Disadvantages are that rope will not always render easily through it, the plunger sometimes won't open far enough without a hard pull on the line (thus making it difficult to snare the guy) and the man on the line has to spare one hand to pull the line while he is guiding the pole to hook the guy.

Trigger Plunger End

This has a plunger like the hand operated piston plunger described above, but it is automatically held in the open position by a catch. When the guy enters the jaws of the end fitting, it presses a trigger which releases the plunger to close the gap thus trapping the guy; the plunger usually has a roller surface to ease movement of the rope. Its advantages are that both hands are available for other work while manipulating the pole, closure is automatic and the rope renders easily. Disadvantages are slight complication of machinery, the trigger can be actuated before the guy enters the jaws (but the plunger can be quickly reset) and real danger to fingers lurks from the powerful plunger if you get in the way.

Bell Mouth End

With a bell mouth end the spinnaker pole is hollow, with either one or two wires running down it, each having a snap shackle at the end where it emerges from the open end of the pole; the inboard end has a rope tail coming out of the side of the pole, with a suitable method of cleating near at hand. The snap shackle fastens round the guy so that it can then be drawn onto the end of the pole by pulling on the rope tail.

Systems of Gybing

There are many permutations of this equipment and we can now examine some of the more common variations, together with the basic principles involved in gybing.

Single Pole, Dipping

This is possibly the simplest basic gybe system there is. The tack of the spinnaker is released from the pole, so that the sail is left to float free under the control of its sheet/guy, the pole is swung forward until it is against the forestay, where it is swung through the foretriangle and clipped onto the sheet/guy on the other side. To get it through the foretriangle, the topping lift must be eased so that the outer end of the pole dips to the deck. If the mast end of the pole is too low on its slide, the pole may be too long to pass behind the forestay, in which case the slider must be pushed up the mast until the pole can dip far enough; the track will usually be marked. The foredeck hand must pull the old sheet, now the guy, inboard so that it can be rove inside the plunger fitting on the outer end of the pole; the topping lift is raised and the pole squared aft for trimming.

(a) ADVANTAGES   The advantages of the single pole dipping system are speed and simplicity, because only one pole, one topping lift, one foreguy and one sheet/guy on each clew is needed.

(b) DISADVANTAGES   Disadvantages of the system are that the spinnaker is without a pole to control it for a short while (this can become exciting in heavy weather, even on small boats; on big ones it is usually only feasible in light conditions, unless a bell mouth spinnaker pole is used so that the new guy can be snared without having to manhandle it into direct contact with the piston plunger at the end of the pole). The headsail sheets have to be remembered in the heat of the gybe, for they must be changed so that the weather one lies over the top of the pole. The system cannot be used with an inner forestay, for the spinnaker pole will not pass through the foretriangle while still fastened to the mast.

Single Pole, End-for-End

This system is nearly as simple as the dipping method outlined above. In essence the sail is released from control by the pole, the foreguy is changed from one end to the other, the other end of the pole is taken off the mast and pushed out to snare the new guy; the first end is then brought into the mast and fastened into the cup or onto the ring.

(a) ADVANTAGES   The advantages of this system are that it is quick and simple (like the dipping system, it does not need duplication of ropes); the topping lift (which should be attached to the middle of the pole so that it works whichever end is attached to the mast) often does not need to be adjusted during the entire operation; it can be used with an inner forestay.

(b) DISADVANTAGES   Like the dipping system, the end-for-end method is best used with small spinnakers or in light weather; headsail sheets have to be slipped off one end of the pole, changed and put back over the other; the foreguy has to be remembered during the gybe; the pole can sometimes take charge when fastened to the spinnaker but not to the mast.

Twin Poles

The basis of the twin pole system is that the new pole is fully rigged in advance, ready to take over completely as soon as the boat has gybed her mainsail. This involves having a second topping lift and foreguy attached, a lazy guy rove loosely through the end of the spinnaker pole jaws to the sail, and the inner end of the pole attached to a second slider on the mast, some time before the gybe starts. At the appropriate moment the pole is topped up, squared partly away and the foreguy set up to allow it to go no further. The spinnaker clew is hauled back into close contact with the end of the new pole, so that the sail is then firmly anchored by two poles, each one controlling one clew/tack of the spinnaker. The old guy is then released from its pole and the spinnaker is trimmed on the new pole to the new gybe; the old pole can be lowered and stowed at leisure – if such a condition ever exists on the foredeck of a yacht racing offshore.

(a) ADVANTAGES   The system can be set up well in advance, so that all is ready for instant action; with the correct lines led aft, a boat can even be gybed with nobody on the foredeck at all. The spinnaker is under complete control at all times because neither clew is allowed to fly under its own volition during the actual process of gybing.

(b) DISADVANTAGES   The twin pole system requires a duplication of all lines: topping lift, foreguy, after guy and sheet. These

108

sometimes require a Houdini to untangle, and use of coloured lines is sensible. In light weather two lines (or a line and a wire) hanging from the free clew of a spinnaker weigh the sail down and produce a poor aerodynamic shape; they must be taken off and a light weather sheet substituted (the tack of the spinnaker is not affected in this way, because the pole takes the weight). If the boat needs to gybe under these conditions, the light weather sheet will not be strong enough to act as a guy and one has to be clipped to the sail before further action can be taken. It takes longer to complete a gybe using this method.

Crewing Tips with Spinnakers

As a crewman, learn all you can about your boat's particular way of gybing. Find out where everything is, which guy or lift cleats where, how the pole ends are fitted and where your station is. Be observant and learn the other fellow's job. Don't let lines off with a rush but develop a rhythm of steady and controlled movement.

Bagging Up

When sorting out a spinnaker to bag it up into a turtle or other quick release container, all you are doing is to work along each vertical side (luff, leech or stay, whichever name you prefer to give it) to see that it is not twisted. Providing these go into the turtle untangled, you can virtually stuff the rest in anyhow and the spinnaker will come out all right; it will help if the foot is also separated and put in first (because it should come out last).

Spinnaker Pole

The jaws of the plunger type end fitting should always open upwards at the outer end, so that the guy can come out easily when required. When easing the after guy to let the pole forward, remember that the guy is not fastened directly to the pole but runs through the end fitting and attaches to the spinnaker. If you ease away with a rush, therefore, the tack of the sail can run out ahead of the pole which may rear skyward; see that the foreguy/downhaul is hauled in at the same time to keep the pole down and pull it forward.

109

Gybing

Don't forget to sort out the headsail sheets when gybing the spinnaker, if you don't want to wind up with one sheet under the pole after the kite is lowered.

Rips

If you spot a small hole or rip in the spinnaker as it is being lowered, tie a loose knot in the sail at that point while you have it to hand. It will save a great deal of searching later.

Hoisting

Up quickly is the watchword if you don't want the spinnaker to fill before it is fully hoisted. Trim the sheet as it goes up, only enough to stop a wrap round the forestay and not so much that it fills the sail before the man on the halyard has finished hoisting. In medium winds and stronger, ease the halyard a foot or two when on a reach so that the top of the sail disengages from the disturbed airflow at the masthead.

Trim

The old tip about having the pole at right angles to the apparent wind still holds good; it can be squared a little more in light winds and eased a bit when it blows up. Never clear the sheet, which should be played constantly to get as much forward drive as possible at all times. Keep the clews level by raising or lowering the pole, except in light airs when the pole may be dropped with advantage (this straightens the luff of the spinnaker and helps it fill at a time when filling at all is more important than aerodynamic shape). Try raising the pole high or dropping it low on a reach if you are also trying to carry a full size genoa at the same time – and only try this on a broad reach. If you are told to square the pole aft, don't forget to ease the foreguy/downhaul as the after guy is hauled in; but don't let it run or the pole may rear skywards and be the devil of a job to get down again.

Rhythmic Rolling

If the boat starts rhythmic rolling, it will be countered by correct trim rather than trying to steer out of it. Harden the spinnaker sheet slightly and ease the pole; see that the mainsail kicking strap or boom vang is pulled well down. You will probably avoid the problem altogether if you use a smaller spinnaker or twin headsails.

Spinnaker Net

If the boat possesses a spinnaker net it should be hoisted whenever the wind is at all light, otherwise the spinnaker will get wrapped round the forestay sooner or later as it collapses from lack of wind. If there is no proper net, a reasonable substitute can be effected by wrapping the tail of the spinnaker halyard round the forestay and the inner stay (if you have no inner stay, make one by leading a line from a suitable point half way up the mast). A genoa or spinnaker staysail can also act as a spinnaker net.

On the Helm

You are unlikely to be on the helm at an intentional spinnaker gybe during your first race but, if you are, there is a lot you can do to help maintain the spinnaker full and drawing. The rudder should be put over at the correct moment with a firm and positive movement, and then taken off again not too soon or too late. The cockpit hand should pull the mainsail amidships at this time, and then move it firmly to the other gybe at the correct time; it should not be allowed to run right off uncontrolled for it may blanket the spinnaker at an inconvenient moment.

Lowering the Spinnaker

If one of the lower corners of a spinnaker is allowed to fly free, the controlled power of the sail is immediately released as it flutters downwind like a flag. If you now give it a lee in which to lower it, the operation becomes relatively manageable.

The usual procedure is to let the pole go forward so that a hand can release the tack and allow the sail to flutter to leeward. The sheet is then hauled in under the main boom until the clew is reached, whereupon the sail can be gathered along the foot and pulled down into the cockpit area as the halyard is lowered. If you are in charge of the halyard, don't let it go with an enthusiastic run, but watch the hands who are collecting the sail as it comes down and don't give them more than they can handle (have you ever tried to gather in a thousand square feet of nylon as it drops into your lap in one lump? You will end up with a most efficient sea anchor, which will stop the boat from seven knots to zero in as few seconds). If your job is to help haul in the sail, keep it out of the water, pull everything you can down and out of the wind, hold it down and avoid dragging it across sharp corners which will tear it.

Halyard and sheet should be unhanked and clipped where they will be easy to find later. This applies more particularly to the halyard, which can easily swing away and aloft if left to itself; the lifeline is a convenient place. If you are taking it forward to clip to the pulpit later, when the boat has settled on a beat, wait until it is on the weather side or you will have to pass it along the lee side of the genoa. Make sure that it is clear outside the cap shrouds as you go forward, or you will twist it aloft and snarl the next hoist. This is especially important at night, when the hand on the halyard may not be able to check aloft properly before he hoists.

Some boats lower their spinnaker by letting the clew fly and pulling the sail down onto the foredeck at the tack. The same principles apply: controlled speed, observation and each man to his allotted task.

Although it is often said that a spinnaker blows out to leeward like a flag when the tack is loosed prior to the sail being lowered, thereby implying that all the strain is off, there is still quite a lot of tension in the halyard. Keep the halyard on the winch or under a cleat until the sail is partly down and some of the weight has been relieved.

When the spinnaker is down any tears must be mended immediately. It must then be packed in its correct turtle or bag, or put into stops, right away. Even if you have a long windward leg in front of you, you never know when you are going to want it again sooner than you think. In any case you may forget that it needs packing properly until the skipper calls for the big one and you haul it out for setting.

8
Watchkeeping, Navigation and Helming

There are those who might wonder how a crewman passes the endless hours of a five day offshore race. The answer is readily apparent if the twenty-four hours are split up.

12 hours on watch
8 hours sleeping
2 hours cleaning ship, galley work and eating
2 hours repairs and general bo'sunry

Watches

It is a surprising fact that many people think that they can go without sleep and stay efficient; this is not so and even an overnight race should adopt some form of watch system unless the crew is young and fit.

The skipper will not normally stand a watch, because he will be required on deck at irregular and frequent intervals throughout the race; he therefore has to take what sleep he can when he can. Similarly it is convenient if enough crew can be carried for the navigator also not to work a watch, being available with the skipper (sometimes the two jobs are combined to advantage) to come up when more hands are required without disturbing the watch below. Some large yachts carry a specialist cook whose rare appearances on deck are state occasions; on others the cooking duties are shared, the owner/skipper perhaps preparing breakfast, lunch being a light meal and supper the main meal of the day, both prepared by the watch below and taken at the appropriate change of duties.

Naval Watches

2000	Midnight	0400	0800	1200	1600	1800
Midnight	0400	0800	1200	1600	1800	2000
First	Middle	Morn-ing	Fore-noon	After-noon	1st Dog	2nd Dog

Most watch-keeping systems are based on traditional naval watches. These are organised into four hour spells, with two dog watches arranged to 'dodge' a recurrence of the same period of duty for the same watch personnel.

Long Watch

2000	Midnight	0400	**0800**	**1400**
Midnight	0400	0800	**1400**	**2000**
		or		
2000	**0200**	0800	1200	1600
0200	**0800**	1200	1600	2000

Two six hour watches in the middle of the day enable lunch to be prepared at 1330 and supper at 1930. If the long watches are kept at night, each crewman has a six hour stretch on watch below and so should be able to get $5\frac{1}{2}$ hours uninterrupted sleep. The snag with this system is the difficulty of maintaining alertness on deck for six hours and, for this reason alone, it is to be viewed with some misgivings.

Swedish Watch

Midnight	0130	0300	0430	0600	0730	0900	
0130	0300	0430	0600	0730	0900	1030	
A	A	C	C	E	E	B	
E	B	B	D	D	A	A	etc.

A crew of five watch-keepers rotates one man every $1\frac{1}{2}$ hours. This system has the advantages of bringing a new man on deck frequently, so that fresh zest is given to the job of getting the best speed out of the boat; there is continuity of watch; only one man is struggling into his gear at any one time. If a third hand is needed the next man on duty is called, so each crewman can expect a minimum of three hours off watch and probably $4\frac{1}{2}$. A large crew, of course, can work the same system in pairs. The main disadvantage lies in the timing of meals.

114

Heavy Weather Watches

If the weather is set for a prolonged gale and the boat is properly trimmed under storm canvas, there is not much to do on deck except steer and keep a good look-out. With a lot of motion on the boat and a good deal of water flying about, this becomes wet and tiring so watches can be reduced with advantage. A good system is to divide the crew temporarily into three watches of two hours each; the duty watch should sub-divide their tasks again so that tricks at the helm are reduced according to the severity of the storm.

2000	2200	Midnight	0200	0400	
2200	Midnight	0200	0400	0600	
A	B	C	A	B	etc.

This system should only be adopted where conditions look set for a period, and a return to normal should be made as soon as the gale subsides or changes character.

Cook Rotation

If a crew of five watch-keepers makes each man cook for a day, with no watchkeeping duties, the cooking is achieved and everybody gets a day off on a long race. This has much to commend it provided everybody can cook – at least there will be variety of fare.

Watch Below Called Early

The watch below will usually be needed on deck when a reef has to be taken in, sometimes to gybe and, more rarely, to change head-sails. Some skippers see to it that those coming up take over cockpit duty while those who have been on watch attend to the reefing, spinnaker gybe or other deck work; they are more wide awake and their eyes are night adapted.

General Crewing

Besides the effort and willingness I have advocated in this book, there are one or two other general crewing principles which should

115

be remembered. Try to keep dry and warm for as long as you can because you will be happier and more efficient if you do so. But you must be prepared to get wet if required, so don't hesitate if a trip forward is necessary in blustery weather; you should have wrapped yourself up earlier.

Once again, keep down unnecessary chatter. It disturbs concentration and wakes the watch below. If another boat is in sight astern don't keep remarking that you think she is gaining on you; don't even keep looking at her or the helmsman will start looking over his shoulder more than at what he should be doing. If the other boat is neither gaining nor losing on you and you are asked how she is doing, try a word of encouragement. If you say that you think you are dropping her, you may well find that it starts to come true in a quarter of an hour or so.

Look-out

Your job may be look-out. This is an important task, particularly when in company with other yachts. When going to windward the genoa turns a large arc of the helmsman's vision into a blind patch, so you should make sure that you check regularly for other boats. At the start, when the whole fleet will be in close company, you may be required to go forward into the pulpit so that a permanent watch can be kept on this blind arc as I mentioned in chapter 3. Offshore and particularly at night make regular checks all round the horizon. If you spot a light at night take a bearing on it immediately; you will want to know as soon as possible whether you are on a collision course with another vessel.

Sail Trimming

Sail trimming is a constant preoccupation while racing. You should be perpetually examining the flow in the sails with a view to improvement. Even with uninterrupted sheet trimming from the cockpit, someone should take a walk round the deck every half hour to look at things from a different angle. Check for incipient chafe, good airflow, sufficiently eased sheets, fairlead angle and that nothing is coming adrift.

Helming and Navigation

These two aspects of crewing are sufficiently specialist to have a section of their own. You won't come up against this problem under difficult conditions too early in your offshore career, so we will leave specific advice for the more general principles later in this chapter.

Weight Distribution

When beating to windward the proper place for the crew is normally the weather deck. If you have no other duty to perform, get up there, get your head down and stay there until you are told to move. There are exceptions to this rather spartan advice: in light winds it may be advisable to heel the boat to leeward a little so that gravity makes the sails take a better shape; in rough weather you will get wet and cold exposed to the waves coming over the top, so you may be ordered to go below and get into the weather berths. At all events, avoid crowding too many bodies into the cockpit area because this will trim the boat aft, which is usually undesirable; the exception is when reaching and there is a tendency to broach as we saw in chapter 5.

Remember when you are on watch, it is both sensible and polite to tell the watch leader, if for any reason you *have* to go below.

Night Sailing

Your first night watch on a dark and windy evening may surprise you. The noise of wind and water is magnified and, even in a force 4, the boat appears to be rushing headlong into space at great speed, with a howling gale blowing about your ears. But this is largely a matter of illusion and, extraordinary as it may seem, gales are not so frequent in coastal waters in summer as they are in the clubhouse bar in winter.

Now is the time when the smaller boats can catch up on their bigger sisters through good preparation and zealous attention to trim. It is not easy to maintain racing keeness during the hours of darkness and he who conscientiously prepares for night sailing and keeps the edge on his crew's zeal will gain hand over fist.

Preparation

As much of the yacht's gear as possible should be recognisable by touch as well as by sight: one button on the sailbag strap of the No. 1 genoa, two on the No. 2 and so on; sensibly arranged lockers and hooks for spare sheets and guys (three hooks on the saloon bulkhead each side of the mast are more readily identified in the dark than an unbroken row of six side by side); notches cut in winch handles to differentiate them; use of laid and plaited ropes where similar sizes could be confusing. All snap-shackles should be of the type with holes for thongs in the plunger ends and they should be properly oiled to make them easy to work. Deck gear and wires must be able to withstand a man's weight if grabbed at in the dark (this means that lazy lines should be made up firmly if stretched along the deck for part of their length). There should be a supply of flashlights with plenty of spare batteries and bulbs (night vision is quick to be destroyed and slow to return, so use them as little as possible and have red screens over some of them); a tilting mirror signal lamp is a godsend for many uses besides morse code messages, such as a mini-searchlight for picking out unlit buoys, or flashing up and down the sails to show motor vessels that you are a slow moving yacht. It is easier at night to see the leeches of a spinnaker with contrasting stripes, to tell if it is pulling properly.

Efficiency

Get a good fix at dusk to give the navigator every chance during the night. The duty watch must not retreat to the comfort and relative protection of the cockpit; stay on the weatherdeck to keep weight forward and up to windward unless it is very cold and wet. Sail trim is just as important as in daylight and the practice of sending a crewman on a trip round the deck at least every half hour should be adhered to. Some skippers make a practice of easing all sheets six inches or so at the change of watches, purely in order to ensure that the oncoming watch is made to trim to the prevailing conditions. It is a good idea to rotate duties within the watch, so that each man has a turn at trimming, look-out and the helm; this makes for variety and keeps interest going. Stopped headsails are easier to set on large yachts and it is easier to stop them before it gets dark. Try changing the spinnaker at dawn if it has been up all night in light airs; a dry one will set better than one covered with dew. It can be difficult at night to spot the moment to kedge; in ghosting conditions be alert to the possibility whenever the current is against you, even if you have to lower the anchor two or three times to check whether you are going backwards or forwards over the ground. Finally, re-
118

member my remarks about the sensation of speed at night. If it blows up, don't be in a rush to reef because you think you are screaming along in a howling gale; take a look at the instruments to check the wind or boat speed, or else check the angle of heel rather than the general sensation on board before you make a decision.

Watch Below

The opposite of 'on watch' is not 'off watch' but 'watch below', because the crew of a yacht racing is never off duty. When you are watch below, therefore, you have other duties besides eating and sleeping, essential though these two are. The most important of these is repairs and general bo'sunry, the second in importance is tidying ship.

Repairs

Nothing must be allowed to stand in the way of repairs. Even if the gear is not wanted immediately, you never know when it will be needed. If you can't use a sailmaker's palm, you can thread needles and wax the twine (if it is not of the ready-waxed kind); you can tidy up a torn sail, mark the repair, dry off the canvas. If you cannot splice wire, you can sort out the rigging to be repaired, get the tool box out, hold a light or get out the correct book to help the rigger at his task. Overhaul that defective winch before it lets someone down badly, whip those sheet ends, clean the speedo impellers, oil headsail hanks and put sail in stops. The list could go on to include the cooking stove, the engine, the head, the bilge pump, steering gear, halyards, spare battens and so on. Hands need never be idle.

Tidying Ship

The smaller the yacht, the more important it is to have a place for everything and everything in its place; this includes boat's gear, food and drink, and your own gear. A continuing battle must be waged to see that all is kept tidy and it is a good idea to have set times for tidying ship. The watch below should tidy up after the night shift before they come on duty at 0800 hours; similarly the ship should be readied for the night twelve hours later. Don't leave bunks untidy, especially if you are operating the hot bunk system of sharing berths with the other watch.

119

Cooking

The cook will always welcome a hand at his duties, especially if you bring some fresh ideas on disguising the inevitable soup and stews. Nobody likes washing up and many hands make light work, so washing up, like preparing vegetables, should never be regarded as the cook's prerogative. Don't overlook the fact that you may have to call on the cook to lend a hand on deck some time; he'll be a more willing conscript if you have previously given him some help at the galley.

Sleeping

So we come back to watches because, when you are watch below, you have a duty to recharge your personal batteries. Make sure that you get your fair share of sleep, or you will become a liability instead of an asset; you will be a burden on your watch mates rather than a positive force in the team. Despite all the other duties outlined above, sleep is important so don't try and do without it.

Navigation

Although you are not shipping as navigator, in common with the rest of the crew you have a duty to help this specialist, particularly when he forms part of a watch and is watch below while you are on deck. First of all, therefore, let us define the duties of the navigator and then see how he can be helped:

1 He must know the yacht's position at all times. He achieves this by dead reckoning (DR) from the log, compass, course steered, tidal information and through fixes.
2 Inshore piloting through eye and navigational aids.
3 Obtaining weather forecasts.
4 Maintenance of all instruments and radio.
5 Provision of information for tactics, including the start, tidal streams, obstacles, wind changes to be expected, angle of the start line, etc.

Yacht's Position

Dead reckoning is the basis on which navigation is founded. Without regular entries in the log sheet, no navigator can hope to achieve an accurate DR position, and it cannot be stressed too much that the duty watch should be conscientious in this chore. Much will depend on the layout of the logbook or sheet which is available, where it is kept and whether the watch master keeps you up to the mark. Be precise in the information you put down and don't, whatever else you do, cheat on the course you claim to have steered. In variable conditions it is best to record the actual course made good at frequent intervals (at least hourly and preferably every half-hour), otherwise it will be hard to estimate the mean course accurately. When you take a trick at the helm, therefore, be honest in your assessment of course made good, even if you show up as a poor helmsman as a result – you will be found out eventually in any case.

When entering the log reading on the log sheet, put down the exact time of reading rather than the nearest hour. If you were busy avoiding a steamer on the hour and subsequently retrimming sails so that you plain forgot, enter the time when you did remember; the navigator won't bless you if you try to cover up.

Never miss an opportunity to take a fix or even a bearing, it may provide the vital confirmation for which the navigator is waiting. This includes back bearings, which can sometimes provide evidence of a tidal set hitherto unsuspected if two or more are taken at intervals.

Inshore Piloting

If the boat is in shallow waters, the navigator will be on deck. Nevertheless, there are ways in which he can be helped. You can draw his attention to a change in the look of the water, you can identify lights, your eyesight may be sharper than others to pick out buoys or even the wording on them.

Weather Forecasts

The duty watch should listen to the radio weather forecasts during their watch. The navigator will usually be around if the weather is changeable, but he may be asleep if you are in settled conditions; write down the forecast wind speed and direction so that there is no possibility of error later. Don't go and panic the navigator out of his bunk just because the forecaster talks of gales – check first on where they are expected, for they may be six or seven hundred miles away.

Instruments

You should have learned about the instruments in your familiarisation period. There is not a great deal you can do to help in their maintenance except to switch off, say, the echo sounder if it is still running when well offshore, to conserve batteries. Even then you should obey the golden rule and ask before you do it (if it has a quirk and won't switch on again without being taken to pieces, you won't be blessed). Know the name of each instrument, its various components and the location of all switches. Make sure that you know how to change batteries, withdraw impellers and switch over to one impeller or the other (i.e. off auto), or to rough from calm or *vice versa*.

'Nip below and switch on the Hound for a second, will you?'

This request should get you moving to the signal amplifier for the speedlog, with the knowledge of how to zero the needle as required. A blank stare will create irritation.

Data for Tactics

You may think that there is little you can do to provide data for tactics, for most of it is available in books, manuals, tidal atlases and the sailing instructions. But the yacht's tactics might well be influenced by other boats in the same race. If you spot another yacht you should do your best to identify her and, indeed, note her course. In addition, the look of the sky can sometimes presage meteorological conditions which might cause a change in wind direction. Note it down in the log.

When to Wake the Navigator

The navigator will often not work a watch, for he will need to be at his duties at iregular intervals throughout the race, particularly at the beginning and end of each leg of the course and usually half way along as a progress check. He has to get his ration of sleep like everybody else, so he will pace himself to suit his needs and will ask to be wakened at specific times unless a major change in circumstances arises.

What, then, constitutes a major change in circumstances?

The yacht's standing orders should set forth theses conditions. They concern anything which calls for a recalculation of course or ETA: a change in wind direction, an alteration of the boat's speed, or a fix or bearing which puts the boat some distance off track. The first, particularly while beating to windward, will mean a new course to steer; the second may mean the same, but will certainly alter the ETA; and the third will mean a re-calculation of course and ETA so that the landfall shall be correct.

Fixes

I said just now that you should never miss an opportunity to get a fix. These can be obtained in a variety of ways with varying accuracy. I won't go into the operation of Consol or any of the other sophisticated aids to navigation which are properly the sphere of the specialist and have their own bibliography. As a crewman, and a new one at that, you will not be expected to serve as second navigator (if you are, you will need more help than I can give you here). But you can and should help by providing useful information on the yacht's position through some of the more ordinary methods of fixing.

Sight Bearings

The most usual form of fixing, apart from sailing alongside a known buoy, is by taking bearings of two or more known points. The most accurate bearing, apart from a transit or range, is one taken with the hand bearing compass. You should ensure that you are relatively isolated from magnetic influences. This includes ferrous ironmongery on your own person (some harness hooks are not guiltless), proximity to large pieces of metal in the boat (the engine, anchor or, sometimes, the lifeline), the steering box if ferrous (galvanised wire is sometimes used in wheel steering gear), the radio and any other electronic device likely to contain magnets, or, more difficult to spot, metal cased (longlife) batteries in the handle of the hand bearing compass itself. Stand well up in the boat to clear such items and to give a better view of the object you are sighting, steady yourself against the movement of the boat to allow the compass time to settle down. At night it is best to try and take the bearing without the compass illuminated and only switch it on to read the bearing when you are happy about the steadiness; in this way you won't destroy your night vision while you are sighting your object. Two bearings give a fix, but if they cut at an oblique angle considerable error can be present; it is better to have two which are nearly at right angles to each other. Three bearings will give a 'cocked hat' and will produce greater accuracy still.

Single Bearings

A single bearing on a light can give a reasonable indication of position on a clear night, if it is taken as soon as the light appears and your height of eye above the sea is known. The chart will show the range at which the light is visible in clear conditions, based on a point of observation 15 feet above sea level; Reed's *Nautical Almanac* gives a table which corrects this to the lesser heights of the average yacht. Be careful not to take the loom of the light for a sighting of the actual light itself. Even without evidence of distance, a single bearing can provide valuable confirmation of position when plotted in conjunction with DR.

Transit or Range

A transit of two lights or a beacon and a headland is a useful and certain position line, which does not even need a compass; it is also 100 per cent accurate. Note it in the log sheet, together with the time, the course being steered and the reading of the log – these three facts are essential items for all entries in the log sheet and never more so than when recording a fix or bearing.

Light Bearings

'It is night time and you are running free on the starboard tack. You see a white (or red or green) light on your port bow. What's the first thing you do?'

This, and many similar questions wrapped up differently, was frequently fired at us by our evening-class instructor in coastal navigation one winter.

'Take a bearing,' we had to chant. And it has drummed it into me ever since.

If the light is the navigation or masthead light of another vessel, you need to establish as soon as possible whether there is risk of collision. If you haven't got the handbearing compass nearby, take a bearing across the yacht's deck, but you will need to make a note of your own heading in this case, so that a second bearing can be taken for comparison with the boat pointing in the same direction. A constant bearing or transit, of course, means that there is risk of collision. Even if the bearing changes only slightly, however, there is little risk of collision if both vesels maintain course and speed, particularly if the other boat is a mile or two off.

Radio Direction Finding

The navigator will know the accuracy of the radio D/F equipment on board; what he won't know is how much faith he can put in the accuracy of your operation of it. Choose a moment when all is relatively quiet and get him to show you how it works. Then try taking a few practice bearings. If you show an interest he will probably be so pleased at the thought of someone else sharing his task that he will be delighted to give you all the help he can. Who knows, you may get a taste for it, in which case you will have taken the first step towards specialisation as a navigator. Members of that union are a dedicated bunch and are always ready to welcome an equally dedicated newcomer. D/F bearings at dusk and dawn are subject to error, as are those where the bearing cuts across the coastline at a fine angle.

Soundings

Depth of water can sometimes provide evidence of position, especially where some other information is available (and it always is, even if only in the form of the DR track). It will usually require specific conditions of shoal water so too much trust should not be put in the answer, but the navigator will know what use to make of your report.

Identification

It goes without saying that the object of any particular bearing should be properly identified. By day one headland can look very much like another in reduced visibility and you should seek corroboration of your opinion. By night the flashing or occulting lights of buoys can be interrupted by waves. Decide on the characteristic of the particular light in question *before* you check it up on the chart; it is human nature to make the flashes fit what you want to see. Learn the meaning of the terse abbreviations which appear alongside buoys marked on charts. If you are looking for a particular unlit object at night, remember that the human eye can see better in the dark at an angle of 15 degrees to the line of sight – so you should look a little to one side of where you expect to see it and it will appear in the corner of your eye.

Meteorology

I have included meteorology under navigation because I shall not be writing enough to fill a chapter on its own, and we have already decided that it is the navigator's job to keep up with the weather forecasts. Part of the crewman's responsibility as far as meteorology is concerned, however, relates to the running of the yacht, particularly where heavy weather is concerned.

The two most important aspects of any weather forecast, as far as a racing yacht is concerned, are wind speed and wind direction; to this end we also want to know the barometric pressure. Of secondary importance is visibility, with rain, temperature and sea conditions tailing off last as only affecting comfort.

You should be alert to radio forecasts, which the navigator will either tune into himself or make a specific request to the duty watch to listen to. The shipping forecasts are the best for yachtsmen, broadcast at specific times each day. The ordinary forecasts as put out at intervals during the day, usually associated with the news, really only concern the landsman and have an infuriating habit of giving everything except the expected wind strength and direction; they are, of course, better than nothing if you have missed the more nautical information aimed at the merchant and fishing fleets.

You should learn the approximate meaning of the Beaufort scale, and the sort of sails you can expect to be asked for in winds of, say, force 6. You can add to your storage of useless information the fact that one metre per second is approximately two knots; it might come in useful in a foreign port if the only forecast obtainable uses the metric system of wind speeds.

The colour of the sky can sometimes reveal the sort of weather to be expected. This is not a certain guide and should only be used as an indicator taken in conjunction with other signs. Black clouds do not, on their own, necessarily presage a storm; red sky at night is not alway a sign of good weather to come. You should note and recognise the general appearance of the sky, the type of cloud, how high it is and whether the visibility is good or bad. A soft sky generally means soft weather and hard clouds mean the opposite – or at least changeable.

High 'mare's tails' blowing across the sky at great altitude usually mean plenty of wind to come, but it may be anything from four to twenty-four hours away, so the sign is not necessarily of immediate use.

The object of this short section, therefore, is to encourage you to place more reliance on the professional weather forecast and less in your own interpretation of the sky. Don't fuss if things look black, it may only be a summer rainstorm.

You may ask how all this affects you. The decisions on reefing, course to steer, whether to order lifejackets and so on are all out of your hands. But you may be asked your opinion before these decisions are taken, and you don't want to establish an early reputation for pessimism. You may, equally, be on watch at dawn when a red sky appears. Should you wake the skipper? The answer is almost certainly no, particularly if the clouds are low and soft. If they are high and dark, possibly with a touch of green in them, then this is another matter and a look at the barometer should tell you. If it has been falling steadily, you can expect worse weather during the morning; if it falls sharply, then you are in for a gale fairly quickly and no time should be lost in telling the skipper.

Rules of the Road

It is the duty of anyone who goes to sea to know the rules of the road. You may be the first man to sight another boat hitherto

127

hidden under the genoa and you should know without thinking whether to shout 'Starboard!' at the boat in question or 'Bear away! Boat on starboard under you!' at your own helmsman, or simply inform him of its presence if there is no danger of imminent collision.

Racing Rules

I'm not saying that you need to be an expert on all the finer points of the IYRU rules (although, if you have raced dinghies, you might well know as much as, if not more than, anyone else on board, and this will help your chances of being asked again). You should, however, know the principal rules and their import, so that you can be trusted to take the helm without the risk of disqualification. The main situations you should master are port and starboard, windward and leeward, overtaking, the meaning of overlap, luffing, use of manual power only, and setting and sheeting of sails. You may, for instance, be ordered to reeve the spinnaker sheet through a block on the end of the main boom. You are allowed to do this without restriction by the IYRU rules but not by the IOR, which limits the distance that a block may be established aft of the outer black band on the boom to six inches.

Some of the important rules are tucked away towards the end of the IYRU rule book. One which affects crewmen specifically is number 66, the last one in part V 'Other Sailing Rules'. It prohibits any member of the crew from stationing 'any part of his torso' outside the lifelines, other than temporarily; so you are not allowed to hang on by your eyeballs perched half on and half outside the weather toe-rail (and a very good rule you may think it is, too). Much depends on the precise interpretation of the word 'torso'; most people take the rule as allowing crews to hang their arms and legs over the lifeline and toe-rail respectively as long as the trunk of their body is inside the lifeline.

International Offshore Rule

As I have shown above, the IOR modifies the IYRU rule in certain respects; it has one specific clause which says that the IOR shall apply where there is conflict. An instance of this conflict occurs where the IYRU prescribes that jib tacks shall be fitted approximately in the centreline of the yacht; the IOR allows a staysail or jib to be tacked athwartships if desired (such as a Tallboy when used off the wind). Another instance is in the use of two spinnaker poles at the same time; the IYRU forbids it except when shifting the spinnaker boom or the sail attached thereto, but the IOR allows it with headails. So the sailing instructions will repay close examination to see that they do, in fact, bind you in the IOR – so will the notice of the race, because the IOR states that this can also commit you to its ruling, even if only by saying that you will be sailing under their handicap system.

Offshore Racing Council

In an attempt to standardise minimum safety requirements, the Offshore Racing Council has issued a series of special regulations on the subject. These are not mandatory but are recommended to clubs organising races under the IOR; it is up to the club concerned whether it adopts any or all of these recommendations, which are divided into six sections: structural features, accommodation, general equipment, navigation equipment, emergency equipment and safety equipment. Races are divided into four categories, each of which has different safety requirements:

1 Races of long distance, well offshore, where yachts must be completely self-sufficient for extended periods of time, capable of withstanding heavy storms and prepared to meet serious emergencies without the expectation of outside assistance.

2 Races of extended duration, along or not far removed from shorelines or in large unprotected bays or lakes, where a high degree of self-sufficiency is required of the yachts but with the reasonable probability that outside assistance could be called upon for aid in the event of serious emergencies.

3 Races across open water, most of which is relatively protected or close to shorelines, including races for small yachts.

4 Short races, close to shore in relatively warm or protected waters.

RORC and NAYRU Special Regulations

The RORC and NAYRU have Special Regulations which supplement the IOR and Offshore Racing Council rules to cover points

129

not otherwise catered for. These include items such as clip points and deck lines, use of retro-reflective material on liferafts and life-jackets, and additional requirements for bilge pumps and other emergency gear.

International Regulations for Preventing Collisions at Sea

At night it is not always possible to recognise that a particular set of navigation lights belongs to another competitor in the same race. The International Regulations for Preventing Collisions at Sea are therefore invoked between sunset and sunrise by most clubs putting on races which last overnight, and yachts must abide by them during these hours of darkness. This immediately brings a different set of rules into force and you should know what they are. The basic ones which affect yachts racing are:

1 Port tack give way to starboard tack.

2 Windward yacht gives way to leeward yacht on the same tack.

3 Power gives way to sail, except where waters are restricted.

4 When two power driven vessels meet head on, each alters course to starboard. When they are crossing, the vessel to port gives way by passing astern of the other. There is no rule as to how a power driven vessel shall avoid a sailing vessel, but she will usually conform to this custom.

5 An overtaking vessel gives way at all times, even when a sailing boat is overtaking a power driven vessel. You are overtaking at night if you are $22\frac{1}{2}$ degrees or more abaft from the other boat's beam (i.e. cannot see the side navigation lights when these are lit). Once you are established as an overtaking vessel, no later change of course alters your duty to take avoiding action until risk of collision is past. In other words you cannot change the situation into port and starboard tacks crossing, simply by a change of course.

6 When a power driven vessel is in sight of another and is taking action required by these rules, she indicates her intentions as follows:

(a) One short blast: I am altering course to starboard.
(b) Two short blasts: I am altering course to port.
(c) Three short blasts: I am operating astern propulsion.

130

7 A vessel with right of way must maintain her course and speed as far as is practical.

8 The fog signal required of a sailing vessel is the same as that required of any vessel towing, fishing or otherwise hampered in her ability to change course rapidly. She must give one prolonged blast followed by two short blasts on her whistle (or foghorn) at least every two minutes.

9 Power driven vessels making way through the water in fog give one prolonged blast every two minutes. When stopped but not at anchor they give two prolonged blasts. When anchored they ring a bell and may also ring a gong and sound · — · on the foghorn every minute.

10 The use of any signal which may be confused with one of the distress signals set forth in the rules is prohibited (see chapter 10).

From the above it will be seen, for instance, that luffing is not allowed after dark, and that there are plenty of instances where right of way is transferred from one boat to the other when the rules change at sunset from IYRU to IRPCS; see figure 21.

This is not all as straightforward as it may at first appear. You may see a port or starboard navigation light on a constant bearing ahead of you. You will know from the presence or otherwise of one or more masthead lights whether it is sail or power driven but, if it is a sailing boat, you will not know immediately whether she is on port or starboard tack; this will have to be established from the wind direction and the course of the other boat (deduced from the sight of one or two navigation lights and their known arcs of visibility).

Ships' Lights

If you are to avoid at night large ships or those carrying out evolutions which make them worthy of avoidance (either by law or common sense), you should know the basic lights of motor vessels. Navigation lights are easy enough, but also at least make yourself familiar with the lights which denote the following:

(a) Vessels engaged in fishing (which must be avoided by law).
(b) Pilot vessels (which can be followed invisibly in thick weather by a large liner).

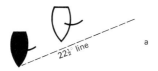

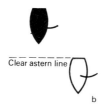

21 *Changes of rules after dark* Under the IYRU rules the white boat has to give way to the black boat as she overtakes to leeward (a). When the black boat is clear astern (b), right of way passes to the white boat and she may sail across the black boat as in (c). At night when the International Regulations for Preventing Collisions at Sea are invoked, the white boat in (a) is deemed to be overtaking because she is more than 22½ degrees abaft the beam of the black boat and cannot therefore see her port navigation light; she thus has to give way. She remains overtaking boat despite the subsequent alteration of the bearing between the two vessels *until she is finally past and clear*, so she cannot luff close across as in (c). The black boat is bound by the rules to keep her course so, should the white boat have decided to overtake to windward, the black boat is not allowed to luff to prevent her.

(c) Vessels engaged in towing (don't try and go between them!).
(d) Vessels engaged in underwater operations (divers or frogmen).
(e) Vessels not under command.

The Navigator

As I have implied, the navigator is an all-important member of the crew of any racing yacht. His calculations can make or mar the race. If he makes a landfall five miles down tide of a buoy, he will have thrown away at least an hour as you struggle to round it; if he is the same amount up tide, you will lose forty minutes even if the wind is free and fresh. So give him all the help you can and don't try and hide any inadequacies of steering or position fixing on your part.

Above all don't argue with the navigator. His task is hard enough already, often performed under difficulties not dreamed of in the dry warmth of a motor cruiser's spacious chartroom. If you doubt the results achieved, you will only undermine the man's self-confidence, disturb his concentration and build in further errors. He has more information to work on than you and, almost certainly, more experience.

The Crew at the Helm

You are sure to be asked to take a trick at the wheel or tiller on a long race. If you have no experience at all, say so and let somebody else do it. If you have ever sailed a yacht or dingy as helmsman then you must be ready to take your turn, or you will be a weak link in the chain if you cannot help out. There are times when you can learn a lot by sitting beside an experienced helmsman and you should take every opportunity to do this, providing you do not disturb his concentration.

You must be prepared to be relieved if the skipper decides that you are causing the boat to lose ground, either through poor windward work or else through not steering a straight or accurate course when off the wind.

The main differences between steering offshore and in coastal waters is that the former places greater emphasis on steering by compass and there is an art to steering a boat in a seaway which cannot be acquired in sheltered waters.

Let me repeat once more the importance of being entirely honest in your assessment of the course you have averaged during your trick at the wheel; you must also report if you find that your average to windward falls below a certain course which the navigator will have given you – it may very well pay to tack if the wind has headed you, and he will need to know if this is so.

133

Windward

Most helmsmen will lay claim to an ability to sail a boat to windward but, although it can be developed, it is by no means possessed by all. Big boats are different from little boats, offshore is different from inshore, a wheel is different from a tiller, but the basic art is the same which, once mastered, will never desert you. You cannot hide inadequacy and must be ready to be found wanting if the skipper decrees that you must surrender the helm; for his part, the skipper must be ruthless in replacing a man who is losing ground unnecessarily to leeward. When you take over the helm on the wind find out what course your predecessor was averaging, free the boat a little and then bring her gradually back onto the wind. Check the course. She will not sit plumb on course offshore any more than she will in sheltered waters, rather less in fact, and you will usually have to sail her marginally more free than you would inshore. In this connection a common fault at night is to pinch. The sensation of speed in the dark will tend to rob you of critical analysis and you will consider that you are roaring along; check the instruments (angle off the wind, boat speed) and keep an eye on the wind tallies in the luff of the headsail. Good windward work requires concentration on the job with no outside distractions. Equally, therefore, you should not as a crewman engage the helmsman in idle talk when you are not on the helm yourself.

Reaching

You may be no good to windward, but there are other opportunities for you to play your part in steering. Reaching in a smooth sea and light winds requires a high degree of concentration on the course to be steered, rather than an inborn ability as a helmsman. You may find that this is your *forte*, and that you will produce a nice straight wake (turn round and have a quick look at it from time to time), with the course averaging exactly the heading given you by the navigator. You must learn to distinguish what is off course and what is the natural swing of the boat as she lifts her stern and sways to the swell. Don't saw away at the helm unnecessarily, trying to steer over the waves all the time, but let her largely find her own way, only meeting her with rudder if she yaws too far. If you can manage this you will be in great demand, because it is not every-

134

body who can concentrate sufficiently to the exclusion of all else.

Spinnaker Reaching

Steering under a spinnaker, particularly in a fresh breeze, is for the experienced only. It requires eyes in the back of your head, an ability to meet the boat without see-sawing on the helm as her counter swings this way and that, an anticipation of any tendency to broach even before it has started, the reticence of a Trappist monk when a snarl-up occurs, and the patience of Job while the foredeck gang tries to sort it out. This is the big time when the loud pedal must be down all the time and races are won and lost, and it quickly reveals any deficiencies in your ability. The distance lost each time the spinnaker collapses is large and it isn't by any means always the sheet trimmer who loses it, particularly on the gybe. A sure hand on the helm under a wildly gyrating spinnaker is worth a lot to an offshore racing crew, and he will be certain of a berth any time he wants one.

At Night

Steering a boat close hauled at night is largely a matter of experience. You cannot see telltales on the headsail without using up a lot of torch battery, and the same goes for wind tallies on the shrouds. If the boat is equipped with electronic wind indicators you will be able to steer a good course without losing anything excessive to leeward. But you must beware of glueing your eyes to the instruments to the exclusion of all else. Development of an ability to beat to windward through feel of the helm and feel of the wind on your cheek takes a certain amount of experience and practice; it comes with the years. With a free wind you are back to a compass course and concentration; try to find a fixed reference point in the sky or on the horizon to use for maintaining your heading, with only intermittent looks at the compass to check (but remember that clouds move quickly so, if you choose one to steer by, you will have to change it soon). You will not only find this less tiring but also better for your night vision.

There is much satisfaction to be derived from a well run yacht making good time on a fair night. The rush of water, the phosphor-

135

escent foam of the wake, the glow of the navigation lights seemingly suspended in two small clouds up at the bow, the comradeship of a shared night watch, all build a picture of quiet efficiency which is good for the soul.

It's not all hell and high water.

9

Ropes and Anchors

Rope work

For racing crews, rope work can be divided into cleating, stowing, knots and repairs.

Cleating

A cleat will usually point at an angle of about 20 degrees to the direction of arrival of its rope or line. This is so that the first turn may be made from the open side, in order that the second does not jam on it when it is put on. The first turn should be a round one, followed by figure of eight turns and finished by a twisted jamming turn or half hitch if the rope is to be made fast semi-permanently, such as with a halyard or preventer. Some owners prefer to finish with a final round turn rather than a half hitch, because of the danger of the latter becoming jammed and thus causing the loss of vital seconds. This is a matter of opinion and I like to use a round turn on sheets but a half hitch on halyards, because I consider that the great danger lies in a line inadvertently coming undone in the slam of a seaway. Find out if your skipper has a preference before you do the wrong thing.

Jam Cleats

There are several jamming cleats which are useful for sheets and guys. Those with spring-loaded cams to grip the rope beside a bullseye fairlead can slip when the teeth of the cams become worn, and they are not as good as those which have no moving parts to go wrong. When using a wedge shaped horn jamming cleat, take a half turn round the blunt end and then jam the rope under the wedge to complete the job; a half hitch is not necessary to finish this off. The same holds good for a horn cleat on the top of a self-tailing winch.

A clam cleat, on the other hand, has a fixed groove with serrated sides, between which the line or rope in question is placed.

Stowing Halyards

Assuming that a halyard is not wound onto a reel winch, it will usually present rope to stow when its sail is hoisted, any wire being limited to the standing part from the sheave to the winch or cleat. The fall, or free part of the line, should be held in the left hand and coiled clockwise with the lay of the rope in the usual way (i.e. towards the loose end so that any kinks work themselves out). The resulting coil will then have to be stowed, usually in one of three ways: in a box or bag near the mast; hanked onto its cleat and/or winch; or trapped under shockcord elastic stretched across the deck.

1 BOX   Each halyard coil should have its own partition in the box, which should be large enough to allow the coil to be laid down without fear of a tangle. See that the coil is turned so that the running end is on top ready to pay out when necessary (xi).
2 HANKED   A bight should be drawn from behind the coil from the cleat, pulled through, twisted and looped over the cleat (xii).
3 SHOCKCORD   Here again turn the coil so that the halyard can run out from the top, before tucking it under the shockcord (xiii).

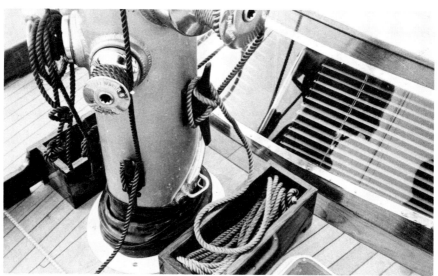

XI *Halyard stowage in a box* When the fall of a halyard is put into a box it should be flaked rather than coiled, particularly if the box is small; it will then run out freely. The cleats on this mast could do with a few degrees of angle to the lead from the winch *Author*

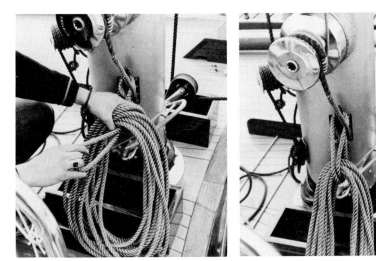

XII *Halyard coiled on a cleat* The bight of rope (a) comes from behind the coil direct from the cleat. It passes through the coil and loops back over the top of the cleat (b). *Author*

XIII *Halyard stowage under shockcord* If halyards are stowed under shockcord they may be coiled and not flaked providing the coil can be stowed flat, but remember to reverse it so that the fall comes from the top. *Author*

Wire Halyards

Where a length of wire has to be made fast and then coiled away before the rope tail is reached (such as on some halyards which allow for the sail to be reefed, or one with a shorter luff to be set), you should not try and cleat the wire direct; this will make a loose job and also tend to kink the wire, with consequent danger of stranding it. It is better to use up the spare wire by coiling it tightly between two cleats or between the halyard winch and a cleat (xiv), before coiling the rope tail as described above. Halyards should be checked at intervals throughout the race to see that they are without tangles and ready to run out if required.

Sheets

Not so very long ago headsail sheets used to be cleated at all times. In the present day search for even the smallest improvement in speed, they are played to suit changes in wind strength. This is particularly important in light conditions to windward, or when reaching.

Even if they are not being played by hand, sheets must be ready to run out at all times. There can be no question, therefore, of coiling or stowing sheets. It is really a matter of tidying away surplus rope from the cockpit area, so that the crew can see what's what. You will find, particularly after the spinnaker has gone up or down, a multitude of lines lying in a mess on the cockpit floor. The first priority is always to get the boat moving at her fastest; sail trim, therefore, takes precedence. When all is settled again, the crew should set about tidying up without further instruction. Coil the loose parts of sheets and guys; do the same for the lazy sheets and guys; turn them so that they are ready to run; stow them in cockpit lockers in the corner of the cockpit or possibly in specially positioned bags on a bulkhead. See that they are out of the way of people's feet and ready for instant use. Some boats make a habit of using ropes of different colours for different use; this greatly helps identification and I cannot understand why it is not more widely practised.

Bosun's Chair

There are one or two points which need to be watched when a crewman is hoisted up the mast in a bosun's chair. If the halyard

XIV *Wire halyard stowage* Wire will not make up directly on a cleat without danger of kinking or coming undone. It should be wound between a cleat and the winch until the rope tail is reached for cleating. *Author*

selected has a snapshackle on the end, don't use it to fasten the chair but pass an ordinary shackle through the eye of the halyard (and have a quick look at the splice as you do so); you don't want the whole thing to come crashing down because the snapshackle plunger has been accidentally tripped aloft – especially if you are in it. If you are using a simple board chair with a rope strop, add a line as high as possible, which can be passed round your back and under your armpits so that you can lean back and still be held in the chair. Take a further length of line aloft to put round the mast when you are up, to stop you swinging like a pendulum if the boat is rolling; this allows you to work with both hands without having to use one to hold on with. The wise man will wear a harness and hook on aloft in really bad weather.

Don't use a plastic bucket to hold tools, for the sides can be pulled in by the weight of the contents thus causing the handle to disengage; a pair of pliers, a hammer and a couple of heavy shackles can do a lot of damage if dropped from 60 feet.

The man on the halyard should see that the line is never taken off the winch while hoisting. In the absence of a winch, there should be

141

XV *To stow a coiled warp* A couple of turns hold the coiled warp in a hank; draw a bight of the free end through the loop; bring it down over the top; pull the free end up through the bight to lock it and form a pendant to tie to a stowage hook. *Author*

XVI *Bosun's chair* This chair is comfortable, has stowage for tools, and is provided with an adjustable back strap and a strap to keep the wearer steady against the mast. *Author*

143

two men on the halyard, one to haul direct and another to take in the slack using a cleat as a fairlead to help hold the weight.

Ease away steadily when lowering, again via a cleat as a fairlead, rather than in short bursts. The man aloft will then have a smoother ride and can come down more quickly, pushing out with his feet as he reaches obstructions like the spreaders, rather as though he were running backwards.

Knots

Bowline

You will probably already be able to tie a bowline but, if you cannot, this is the one knot which you must master forthwith. You must know it so well that you can tie it with one hand, in the dark, or where you cannot properly reach, even under water. It is the nearest thing to the all-purpose knot and is a vital piece of know-ledge in your qualifications as a crewman. Like all good knots, the bowline will not slip and it is easy to tie once you have mastered it; it also has the very desirable quality that it can be readily undone because, while it locks under strain, it does not jam. The method of rabbit-running-round-a-tree is useful to landsmen but requires two hands and too long; you should learn the seaman's way as in figure 22.

There are other knots which are based on the same principle as the bowline, where the load on the standing part locks a half hitch through which a bight of the rope has been passed. A double ended headsail sheet can be fastened to the clew of the sail by means of a bowline on a bight, with the free ends passed through the bight; figure 23.

An alternative method, again based on the locking principle, is to have a short line attached to each headsail clew and to form a sheet bend with it as in figure 24.

Reef Knot

The reef knot is easy to learn and is to be preferred to the overhand, or granny, knot for many purposes besides reefing. The left-over-right-and right-over-left method is a good way of memorising the reef.

144

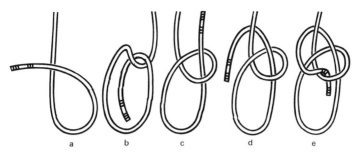

a b c d e

22 *Bowline* Hold the standing part of the rope in the left hand, palm upwards, and take the fall round in a loop above the standing part, with the right hand palm downwards where they cross (a). Twist the right hand down and towards you so that the fall is pushed down over the standing part and up through the loop; the fingers of the right hand should now be turned towards you, palm uppermost, with the fall through the loop and the standing part beginning to form a half hitch (b). Transfer the left hand to the standing part above the half hitch and flick the fall underneath the standing part and out through the loop (c). The fall is then taken by the left hand round the back of the standing part (d) and pushed down through the loop (e); the bowline is now loosely formed. Draw the knot tight by pulling on the standing part and *both parts* of the fall (not the loop or the knot may capsize).

Rolling Hitch

I have not included the half hitch as such, because this is such a simple manipulation of a rope that it comes as second nature to most seamen. The rolling hitch is a useful variation which prevents a hitch from slipping along a pole or other line which is under tension. Figure 25 shows how this should be tied, and it should be noted that the second turn round the pole or line is taken on the side towards which the slip is expected.

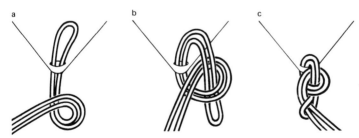

a b c

23 *Bowline on a bight* The bight of the doubled sheet is passed through the clew, through the half hitch and both ends of the sheet are then passed through the bight. This knot is easily undone without a spike and does not catch on shrouds when tacking.

145

Figure of Eight

The final commonly used sailing knot is the figure of eight. This is used at the end of a sheet or halyard to prevent it escaping through a fairlead or mast sheave. It is preferred to a single overhand knot because the result is slightly larger.

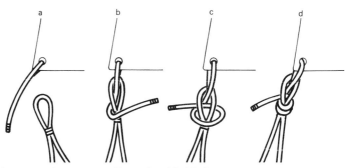

24 *Sheetbend on a clew pendant* To make this hitch more secure, use two passes of the pendant round the back of the loop of the sheet instead of one.

Tarbuck Knot

Partly because I would hate any old salts who might pick up this book not too find anything new in it. I have included the Tarbuck knot which I will wager not many will have met in precisely this form. Mountaineers have used synthetic ropes for a long time and we can take a few tips from them without loss of face; after all, they have borrowed the bowline from the sea. The Tarbuck knot was developed specially for use with nylon rope and is designed to hold under all but severe shock load, yet still to be free enough to be adjusted by sliding the knot along the rope. It is suitable for kicking straps, taking the strain off a sheet while moving the lead or clearing a riding turn on a winch etc; see figure 26.

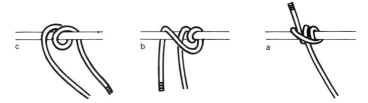

25 *Rolling hitch* Take two turns round the spar or rope on which it is desired to make a knot, and finish off with a half hitch opposite to the direction against which the pull is expected.

26 *Tarbuck knot* The turns are all taken round the standing part in the same direction, three along the line and the fourth at the opposite end; a fifth turn is taken (still in the same direction) round the part of the rope where it crosses back over the first three turns, but this turn is not also taken round the standing part as well. The end is pulled tight back once again across the first three turns to lock the knot.

Splicing

A simple eye splice is a useful accomplishment, which the experienced crewman should be able to achieve. Synthetic rope has a tendency to go a bit hard after a certain amount of use, and is then liable to close up again quickly if a conventional marlin spike is inserted and removed from the lay. A scooped splicing tool makes the task much easier, as it can be left through the lay while the strand is tucked. I have used a form of large crochet hook for splicing with advantage and wonder that it is not more widely practised. You are not likely to be called upon often to do a long or short splice, so there is no need to get involved at this stage; if you find fascination in the work, there are books devoted to the subject of rope work which will enable you to do crown knots, turk's heads and all the allied knots and splices.

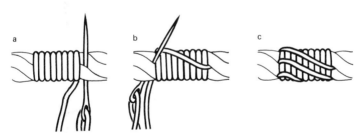

27 *Sailmaker's whipping* A plain whipping, which has its ends tucked under half a dozen turns at each end, has a tendency to come undone if the final turns are by chance scraped off the end of the rope. A sailmaker's whipping will last indefinitely, because the free end of the twine, after being sewn between the strands of the rope with a needle, is carried back across the serving along the lay of the rope, sewn through the strands again and brought back to the other end, where it is again sewn through and brought to the other end along the third lay of the rope. In this way the whipping is held fast on the rope and the turns will not pull off.

Whipping

An ordinary whipping will soon pull off in the normal wear and tear of working the ship, and it is almost a waste of time to put it on. You should get hold of a sailmaker's needle and see that the whipping is held in place by laying the thread over the serving and sewing through the lay of the rope (fig 27).

Anchoring

I do not propose in this book to go into the whole question of anchoring, since the subject can become lengthy and involved. You should, however, know the basic principles involved and be able to contribute to the solution of some of the more common problems likely to be encountered.

The average yacht will have a bower or main anchor and a kedge anchor; she may easily have a third if she is larger than 30 feet overall. There are three main types of anchor as follows.

Fisherman

The old fashioned anchor, with two flukes and a collapsible stock at the other end of the shank, is known as a fisherman or admiralty type. When the anchor reaches the seabed and is pulled along, the stock ensures that one of the flukes is directed towards the ground where it digs in until the shank and stock are lying flat on the bottom. A fisherman does not have the same holding power as more modern designs and suffers from the fact that one fluke is always sticking up out of the seabed. If the boat catches her anchor rode (*rode*: chain, wire or rope used for anchoring a vessel) round the exposed fluke as she swings to the tide, the anchor becomes 'foul' and can pull itself out. It is wise to give the boat a bit of sheer if lying to a fisherman, so that she swings clear when the tide turns.

Ploughshare or CQR

This is shaped as it name implies, but it is really a *double* plough-share so that it wedges its way in; it has no stock. As the anchor is pulled along it tips on its side, the blade of the ploughshare digs in and the anchor rights itself as it bites into the seabed. It has many times the holding power of an equal weight fisherman and it also

148

digs right in leaving nothing exposed to catch on the rode. On the other hand it is rather lumpy to show, can capsize under certain circumstances and is not at its best in weed or coral.

Parallel Fluked

The pioneer parallel fluked anchor was the Danforth, since copied or independently developed by others. The anchor works in a similar manner to the stockless anchor used on warships, with two or more parallel flukes shaped and pivoted to dig in easily; it has the important addition of a stock across the crown to ensure that it lies flat when digging in. Here again we have many times the holding power of the fisherman and there are no exposed parts to snag on the rode. The very efficiency of the anchor, however, means that it can bury itself completely in soft mud and can be the very devil to break out again.

Other Types

There are several other anchors, each having its own use. The mushroom type is shaped as you would imagine, like a mushroom; its principal use is as ground tackle for a line of mooring chains (good holding power but an awkward shape). The grapnel is generally three or four pronged and a much more lightweight affair; it is most often seen on trailer-boats or daysailers, but you might come across one in use as a racing kedge. A relative newcomer is the Bruce anchor which has three flukes scientifically shaped to dig in and hold. It is generally lighter than others of equal holding power, and is becoming very popular.

Chain

The traditional rode for anchoring is chain. It confers a certain amount of holding power of its own, due to its weight but, above all, it ensures that the pull of the boat on her anchor is horizontal along the seabed. Chain is strong and virtually impervious to chafe or wear over the periods we are considering. Its main drawback is lack of elasticity, but it can be given this through catenary action. The usual scope of chain is three times the depth of water at high tide. Chain is easily stowed if a suitable locker is arranged under a navel pipe, as it falls freely into folds under its own weight.

149

Nylon Rope

Nylon rope offers the advantage of elasticity, which confers great capacity to absorb shock loads. Further advantages lie in economy and lightness. The latter, while it makes for ease of handling, means that a short length of chain is needed next to the anchor to ensure that the pull is horizontal; this has the double effect of removing nylon from the seabed where it may be subject to chafe on rocks. Where three or four fathoms of chain are used with an otherwise all nylon rode, the usual scope to pay out is four to five times the greatest depth of water. Nylon is hard to wash mud off and is awkward stuff to handle on deck; it is best stowed on a reel or coiled into its own container. It should be protected from chafe where it passes through any fairlead. Its elasticity makes it take longer to break out an anchor, as a firm pull is not transmitted to the seabed until the stretch has been taken up.

Polyester Rope

Terylene or Dacron rope is rather like nylon, except that it does not have quite as much inherent stretch. This means that it cannot absorb as much shock load as nylon and is therefore not so suitable as a main anchor rode. On the other hand a kedge anchor used in racing is usually only required in calm conditions and often has to be broken out quickly; polyester is therefore preferable under these circumstances.

Wire Kedge Line

You may meet an owner who carries a long, thin wire kedge line for the occasions when you are caught in an adverse tide and no wind in really deep water, when the effect of the tide on a rope line nullifies the holding power of the kedge. The wire *must* be kept on a coil, and the anchor will not hold unless you veer wire to at least three times the depth of water. Whether it is worth carrying the considerable weight of wire for the rare occasions it may be used is a debatable point, and both paying out and hauling in is tricky.

Kedging

Your most likely use of an anchor while racing is to kedge. In this case the conditions will probably be no wind and a calm sea, together with a full crew as anchor watch, so almost certainly you will use a fairly light anchor with a polyester line, possibly with two or three fathoms of chain. The racing rules do not allow you to throw the anchor forward, so you drop it over the bow or stern and then pay out rope until you feel it bite; allow a little more for security and then make fast. It is worth noting at this stage that the racing

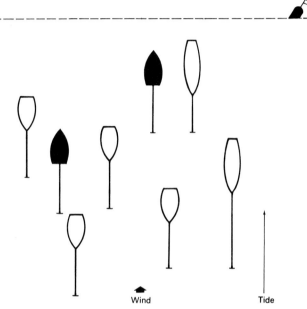

Wind   Tide

28 *Kedging over the stern* All boats have kedged short of the starting line to avoid being carried over in conditions of more stream than wind. At the gun, the black boats can hoist their spinnakers and trim sails for the course before weighing anchor, because they only have to haul their kedges over the stern to get under way. The white boats have to pull up their anchors and turn round with little, if any, way on before hoisting their kites.

rules give right of way between two boats at anchor to the one which anchored first (this may become important if one drags onto the other), so don't waste time if you are in a fleet all of which are kedging and, equally important, make a written note of those boats which kedge after you. When the time comes to weigh anchor, pull in with a will to get the thing broken out and on board quickly; if the wind has got up, the helmsman will want to get sailing again as quickly as possible.

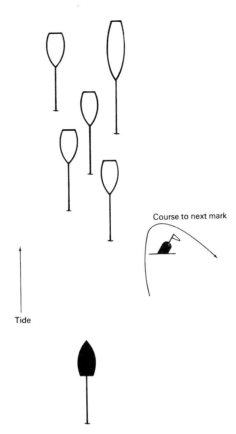

29 *Kedging over the stern* The white boats have all gone downtide past the mark before kedging by the bows, pointing back in the direction they wish to go when the wind freshens. The black boat has kedged over the stern short of the mark, also pointing in the direction she wishes to go. When kedges are raised, the white boats will all tend to drop astern on the tide as they slowly gather way to fetch across the tide; the black boat will gather speed through the water as she drifts towards the mark and should have enough way on to be able to cut it close by the time she reaches it.

Main Anchor

If you are anchoring in a port after racing, care must be taken in selecting a site; you don't want to pick up mooring chains or submarine cables. It is usual to let go and then drop astern either under action of the current or motor. A second anchor is sometimes put out, either by dropping double the distance astern you reckon to lie, then letting go the kedge and pulling up on the bow anchor, or else

152

by putting it out in a dinghy; this restricts your circle of swing to about half that required for a single anchor. So that the boat may swing properly, see that both anchor rodes are joined, and the join lowered so that it lies below the level of the keel to stop one or other of the rodes getting caught round the rudder; the boat is then said to be moored rather than at anchor. If you are using nylon rope for either anchor, see that it is parcelled with rag or a piece of sailcloth to guard against chafe where it passes through the fairlead.

Tripping Line

To ensure that you can get the anchor up again without trouble, even if you hook an obstruction, a light tripping line should be made fast to the crown and either buoyed or brought aboard. If the anchor gets under a cable or chain on the bottom, you can then pull it out forward by heaving on the tripping line.

Clearing a Snagged Anchor

If the anchor seems irretrievably snagged on the bottom, try to sail or motor it out first. Make up over the exact spot, shortening the rode as you go, until you have little room for movement, then swing the bow from side to side as you go ahead. If this fails, you will have to resort to sterner stuff, almost certainly involving the use of your second anchor. Remember to fit a tripping line to this one so as not to be caught again. There are two basic ways of going about the job. First, make a collar by using a short length of chain shackled to each end of a ring spanner, or else tie a line across the flukes of a dinghy anchor (even an empty can suitably weighted is better than nothing) and allow this to carry a line down the chain and over the shank of the anchor, thus to become a makeshift tripping line when pulled forward from the dinghy. This will only work with stockless anchors so, if you have a fisherman down, you will have to use another method. Haul in as much as you can on the anchor in order to lift the snagged mooring chain or cable off the seabed (you may even get it near enough to the surface to see it and get at it). Then try to hook the same cable with your second anchor, haul this tight as well, lower away the snagged anchor and pull it clear forward (possibly using a line on a collar as described above). Finally remove your second anchor by means of its tripping line.

Fouled Anchor

In the event of an anchor and chain absolutely refusing to come up, haul in as tight as the rode will come, fasten a stout line as long as the depth of water to a link in the chain, and put a buoy on the other end of the line. Then cut the chain inboard of the new attachment with bolt croppers, hacksaw or cold chisel and hammer. You can now come back at a more convenient time to recover anchor and chain, or ask a yard boat with powerful hoisting tackle to do it.

General Anchoring Tips

This is not meant to be a book on cruising and you must buy one of those if you want to go deeper into the subject of anchoring, but a few practical hints may be of use. If you are having trouble breaking out an anchor, try hoisting it with a halyard or sheet winch before resorting to the more complicated methods suggested above. A boat which is snubbing badly to her chain can be eased if a weight of something between 40–100 lb is lowered on a ring or big shackle round the rode via a line, to a point about one third of the way towards the main anchor. Use of brass or bronze near to galvanised iron will eventually remove the galvanising through electrolytic action, so avoid brass or bronze shackles. Do not use a half hitch when making fast a chain to a sampson post or mooring cleat, for it will be difficult to undo; you should take a bight of the chain,

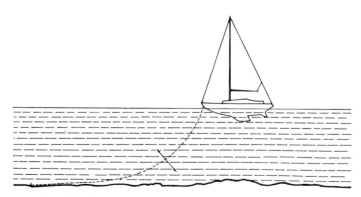

30 *Catenary action* The long bight of an anchor chain as it hangs in a curve from the anchor on the seabed to the bow of the boat will absorb shock loads through catenary action. The bight rises and falls as the boat surges backwards and forwards or pulls at the chain due to action of the waves.

pass it under the standing part and then loop it over the sampson post. Don't forget to see that the rode is made fast at both ends before anchoring; you may scoff, but many an anchor chain has snaked gaily over the side to disappear for ever. Remember that races have been won before now by the use of the kedge.

10
Bad Weather and Emergencies

Bad Weather Precautions

Some aspects of this chapter have already been dealt with in previous pages, but it is convenient to collate all the information in one place and a little repetition will do no harm.

The days are gone when it was considered the proper seamanlike thing for a yacht racing to heave to and lie aback or a-hull and ride out a gale to a sea anchor. Modern sailing vessels are well balanced and well found, the race is still on, so keep her going in all but the most severe gales.

When to Reef

It seems to be generally agreed that most yachts reef too late and shake them out too late (perhaps this is the result of taking too much advice from books like this about not panicking when black clouds appear). If you are running free as the wind gets up, it is easy to fail to appreciate just how strong it has become. Let us assume that the relative wind on the boat is 15 knots and that you are travelling at 7 or 8 knots; a nice breeze and a good speed. You are running away from the wind, however, and its actual speed is 22 or 23 knots. When you come on the wind at the turning mark, the relative windspeed will be nearly 30 knots as you punch your way into it.

You will do as you are told but, if there is a choice and the signs are right for strong winds, you will make a better job of reefing before it becomes too windy; the effect on crew morale will also be good as the canvas rolls in. But remember my earlier warnings against succumbing to the false sensation of increased wind strength at night and about taking every dark sky for a gale warning: you have to be certain that the signs are right before you take action. Equally you should be ready to put on more sail as soon as the storm shows signs of abating. When the wind is dying down it is tempting to think that the boat is already doing her maximum speed, so what is the point of pressing her with more canvas? In any case you are tired and wet. But it is in the lulls that the speed drops off, even momentarily, and it is for these that you require more sail. There will still be gusts of extra severity and these will lay the boat well over, but the lulls will pass by almost unnoticed to start with as they are of such short duration.

Be ruthless. Even though it is near the end of your watch, force yourself to suggest more canvas now rather than leaving it for your reliefs to do when they come on in an hour's time. In this way the watch master may be goaded into waking the skipper for his opinion, which will almost certainly be to increase sail if the wind shows signs of abating.

Harness

If it is necessary to reef you *must* be wearing a harness, whatever the boat's standard harness orders.

Personal Buoyancy

The operative word here is 'personal'. Everybody has his likes and dislikes, and my own preference is for a mouth inflated air lung incorporated into a sailing jacket. This is because it is less bulky than any kind of permanent buoyancy, either solid or air cells. I wear it at all times when it is likely to be needed and it also acts as an insulation against the cold if it is kept partly inflated (when it is also ready to help keep me afloat should I fall overboard). The drawbacks of this kind of buoyancy are a complete reliance on air inflation by mouth without any automatic system and a danger of a puncture from chafing or cuts; but I have it religiously serviced at the start of each season. Many yachts have for each crew member air lungs pure and simple, which are strapped on when precautions have to be taken and which are inflated by a small gas cylinder. These take up little room but have two minor drawbacks: they are not always easy to put on quickly in the dark and you can never be certain that they are fully operational. Permanent buoyancy (kapok and the like) is difficult to stow and bulky to wear; it often makes you sweat. Whatever type you use, make sure that it is serviced regularly, for your life may depend on it one day.

Main Boom Preventer

When reaching or running in a gale, you should consider a boom vang or else a preventer; a line or wire from the outer end of the boom, led forward to a strongpoint on deck and lashed down. It is designed to prevent the boom from working back and forth and, indeed, from gybing accidentally. Special care should be exercised by the helmsman when running dead before the wind because, while the preventer stops many an accidental gybe, if the worst does happen, it would become a serious menace as it holds the boom back while the rest of the mainsail slams across. It is for this reason that many cruising men prefer a trysail to a Swedish mainsail for the really strong stuff; the main boom can be lashed amidships with a trysail, which sets loose footed. The Swedish mainsail is closer winded than a trysail, but needs the boom to make it work.

Storm Canvas

If your boat is properly found she will, therefore, have a trysail or a Swedish mainsail. She will also have a separate track on which this sail can be bent while the mainsail is still set; this track will be low on the mast, with a gate like a set of model railway points, so that the mainsail can be lowered on its own normal track and then the trysail hoisted in its place from the 'siding'. Some owners are sufficiently pessimistic to guard against failure of the mast track, by wisely ensuring that the trysail slide eyelets are made large enough to receive a lashing; parrel beads can thus be rove as well as or instead of the slides. Your early reconnaissance should have told you where all this gear is stowed.

For the average summer gale encountered in most inshore waters, however, you will probably make shift with a double reefed main-sail, or between five and eight rolls of the roller reefing. You can't learn to reef an offshore racer in gale conditions from a book (heaven preserve you if you are caught in a gale with a crew who has to turn to you for guidance on your first trip when they want to reef). But you will want to know here what your duties are likely to be. Most damage to sails is caused in gales by loose canvas flogging when head to wind or badly stowed; be quick, and keep a clear deck.

Jiffy Reefing

Jiffy reefing is quick; it is also efficient. It has evolved because modern sailcloth is strong enough to withstand gale conditions even though it is only attached at tack and clew. This does away with the need for multitudinous individual reef points all along the boom. Somebody also gave a little thought to simplifying the traditional reefing system.

The gear should be permanently rove, so that everything is always ready to be used. The sheet and halyard are eased, the luff lowered so that the new tack cringle can be slipped over a hook positioned at the gooseneck, the reef cringle at the leech is pulled down to the boom by the reefing line to form the new clew, and the mainsheet is hauled in again. The loose foot of sail lying in a fold along the boom can be tidied up later by the use of reef-points or a lacing, but this is only really necessary if the gale is severe or the reef likely to be held for long. The essence of the system is that the clew should pull along the boom as well as down, when the reef is in. It is therefore important that the reefing line at the outer end of the boom should run via a fairlead which is just aft of the position of the clew in the reefed position. In practice, this fairlead may well be adjustable and its position marked on the boom. The system will usually be duplicated for the second reef, and there will probably be a much smaller one to act as a flattening reef without reducing area.

Roller Reefing

For some time roller reefing was the quickest method of reducing the size of a mainsail. Usually operated by means of a handle turning a worm gear at the gooseneck, the result gives an indifferent shape to the reefed sail. Watch out that you don't drop the handle overboard in the general bustle.

If your boat is engaged in rolling down a reef and, being a newcomer, you have no specific task other than general help, you will want to contribute more than fetching and carrying the reefing handle for the man who is working at the goose neck. The extra cloth at the luff end of the sail, which normally forms the belly or flow near the mast, will bunch on the boom in an untidy mess if left to itself. It is surprising the number of owners who do not take

159

elementary steps to combat this. Stuff a couple of sailbags or some teatowels into the forward end of the roll as it goes, and the bagginess will be controlled (but don't forget them when you unroll or you may lose them overboard). Secondly, don't forget the special kicking strap vang which some boats carry for use when reefed. This is a length of Terylene webbing with an eye worked into one end; the plain end is rolled in with the sail to leave a foot or so of webbing hanging down when the roll is complete. The kicking strap can then be attached to the eye and used normally.

There is always room for another hand to pull the leech well aft as the boom is rolled. This helps the set of the finished sail and sometimes needs a good deal of strength.

Through-mast Roller Reefing

Some boats roll their boom by means of a handle fitted in a socket at the front of the mast. This turns the boom by means of a direct drive which goes through the mast. To allow this, the gooseneck cannot travel up and down on a track, so it is fixed in the vertical plane.

Having no gears, the system is simpler and, indeed, much quicker than a conventional roller. It suffers from the normal drawbacks of any roller (poor sail shape, possible gear failure, and danger of losing the handle), but its speed means that it can also be used in order to stow the mainsail without folds by rolling it round the boom.

Points or Lacing Reefs

If the boat has neither jiffy nor roller reefing, then you will probably be in for a tedious struggle as you reeve lines and tackles. I won't go into it all here, except to say that the various lashings should normally be kept in a special bag, and the temptation to use them when looking at other times for a relieving tackle or an extra length of line must be firmly resisted. The gear must also be put back when shaking out a reef, or you will be in trouble when you want it again in a hurry.

When shaking out a reef, make sure that *all* points are untied before letting go the clew and tack lashings, or the sail will tear.

160

Headsails

The ORC Special Regulations recommend that any storm jib designed for a seastay or luff-groove device should have an alternative method of attachment to the stay, or else a wire luff so that it can be set flying should the groove be damaged. Even if the jib is hanked on, a stout shackle should be added at the head and tack, and shackled to the forestay, because the piston hanks are the weak links in this particular chain. Here is a job for the unemployed at this time. It is possible that the working jib will double as a storm jib by having a row of reefing points. These tie under the foot of the sail just as they would on a mainsail. When gybing with the storm jib in a gale, keep both sheets on the winches and haul them both in as hard as possible.

Jib as Trysail

Some boats do not carry a trysail, but have a row of stout eyelets worked along the foot of a suitable headsail. This allows the sail to be bent to the mast by means of a lacing, so that the leech becomes the loose foot of a trysail which is then sheeted from the head with the main boom stowed.

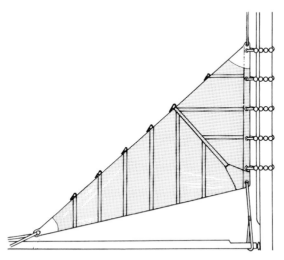

31 *Jib as trysail* The foot, reinforced with tape, becomes the luff and is fastened to the mast with parrel beads.

I remember racing a 30 footer round the cans one day in the sheltered waters of southern England. We were beating to windward under mainsail and genoa when we were hit by a summer squall too suddenly to give us time to tie down a decent lacing reef; the wind rose from 15 to 55 knots in as many seconds and the local weather station later reported gusts of 70 knots. We dropped the mainsail altogether and continued under full genoa beside another boat which did the same; both yachts behaved extremely well although the poor genoas were never the same again. When the moment arrived to tack to clear the shore on our lee, we had three goes at it. Fortunately I had decided to tack in plenty of time, for we finally had to gybe right round the other way. A dropped mainsail on a yawl or ketch makes a first class quick reef under these circumstances, because the boat remains well balanced; if you drop the mainsail of a sloop or cutter you will have all your sail area forward, so remember to leave yourself enough sea-room to gybe if you have to go onto the other tack to clear a headland.

RORC Gale Recommendations

In 1956 some 23 yachts were caught in a severe gale in the English Channel while racing. Fortunately there were no fatalities to the crews, although another yacht cruising in the area lost three out of the four people on board. The RORC was able to evaluate the reports from all the yachts, together with those of the various rescue services and the weather experts; the result was a paper which contains some useful recommendations. These should be examined in detail by all owners and skippers; only those more pertinent to crews are summarised here.

1 The navy adage that it pays to have plenty of sea-room in a gale still holds good for offshore racers.
2 For those yachts with plenty of sea-room, there appeared to be no preference for heaving to, lying to a sea anchor from the bow or the stern, lying a-hull, or streaming warps ahead or astern.
3 Most damage to sails was caused by flogging.
4 The value of safety harnesses was stressed.

Adlard Coles, in his book *Heavy Weather Sailing*, examines this gale along with many others and has some useful hints to offer.

Do not leave a headsail lashed in a bundle on deck when it has been replaced by a storm jib. Heavy weather will soon tear it loose and carry other gear away.

A trick at the helm should be reduced to fifteen minutes.

When streaming warps it is quite possible to have too much over the stern. This reduces speed to such an extent that the boat retains little steerage way, thus making it difficult to keep her stern on to the breakers.

There is no uniformity over an area in the strength of gales which can, in fact, be quite local.

Turbulent gusts cause breaking cross seas which are liable to hit from unexpected directions. If these are aggravated by steamer wakes or tide rips caused by a shelving or uneven seabed (rocks or wrecks), the effect can be spectacular and dangerous to crew on deck.

Man overboard

It seems logical at this point to go more fully into what action should be taken if a man goes overboard. It is obvious that the problem is minimal if he is wearing a harness and still attached to the boat, so this is the first point to make: always wear a safety harness and hook on in difficult conditions.

As soon as anyone goes over the side, call all hands on deck with the traditional cry of 'Man overboard!' This lets everyone know that he must come up immediately, exactly as he is without waiting to dress; you should throw a lifebelt at the same time.

One hand should be told off to keep an eye on the man in the water at all times, with no other task to distract him. This is important, for a human head is small and can quickly be lost among the waves. The skipper will take charge and decide what action is to be taken. Much will depend on course, sails and conditions, but generally a smart gybe and return will not be possible right away. If the spinnaker is up, a good way to get it down quickly is to cut the halyard, as it then falls into the water without causing a bag; there is a slight danger that the halyard will knot itself as it snakes aloft and so defeat the object, so a little extra time taken to undo the halyard and pay it out may be worth it. But ease sheet and guy immediately to slow down and reduce the distance you must go back. Obviously it will help to have the engine running, even if you don't use it, so get this going quickly. Secondly, leave a trail of cushions, boxes, bottles and anything which will float and so mark the way back. If you are on the helm, take a reading of the compass, hold your course steady and note the time. When you are relieved by the skipper or owner (as you almost certainly will be) tell him the course you have been on since the man fell in and that you have kept it steady for a precise number of minutes or seconds; this may remind him to do the same, when his mind will be full of others things. With this knowledge, a reciprocal course can be steered to bring you back within a close distance of where the man fell overboard.

If you are the unlucky one who goes over, grab at anything – contact with the boat is vital, even for a few seconds. If a log line is being trailed, swim for it; it probably won't hold you for long at high speed but it might. When all contact is lost, tread water and keep calm. If you are wearing a lifejacket you should be able to float easily until the yacht returns to you; it is not worth wasting your energy trying to remove seaboots or oilskins. If you have no lifejacket, you will know your own swimming ability best and the state of the sea will soon tell you whether you can shed clothing easily (seaboots usually fit closely and are not easy to remove in water). I always carry a whistle and, indeed, a small pack of distress rockets, in my oilskin jacket (which also has buoyancy and a compact harness built into it – sometimes I think that I will eventually be drowned by the weight of my safety equipment, but any fool can drown and it sometimes takes an intelligent man to say alive); certainly a plastic whistle is easy come by and may one day save your life.

When the boat finally returns to the man in the water, she should shoot head to wind just as though she were picking up a mooring. Have a line ready with a loop in the end, knotted with a bowline so that it can be passed over the man's head and shoulders to help him aboard.

Damage Control

Much of what you can achieve if the yacht is damaged will depend on the nature of the equipment available. The most important single item of damage control gear, not counting a fire extinguisher, is a pair of stout bolt croppers or a hacksaw.

Collision

If you are in collision with another yacht, don't try and fend off with your hands or feet except at very slow speeds. Even two five tonners coming together carry a lot of momentum and you are only going to add a crushed foot to the problem if you try and shove off her toe-rail. If you are on the helm while all this is going on, keep the relative speeds down by turning onto the other boat's course as much as possible; this usually means that both yachts should luff rather than try to bear away under the other's stern.

Dismasting

If your mast goes overboard, then you have to recover it, lash it on deck and motor home. If you have no bolt croppers, this usually means a painstaking undoing of turnbuckles or toggles which can be difficult in a seaway, so don't forget to hook on. If there is no danger of drifting ashore or of anyone being washed overboard, then obviously undoing the rigging rather than cutting it will save the owner money. At all events, see that every last wire and rope is safely on board before starting the engine, or something will inevitably get caught round the propeller.

Jury Rig

Another reason for retrieving all you can of a broken spar is that you may want to use it later to establish a jury rig. A length of mast, the boom or even the spinnaker pole can often be lashed to the stump of mast which is left sticking out of the deck, stayed fore and aft and athwartships, and used as a makeshift mast to set a small steadying sail.

Steering by Sails

If the steering mechanism fails in such a way that the rudder swings idly or is fixed near to the centreline, you can keep the boat on course by means of sails: pulling in the mainsail will make her luff, the same on the headsail will make her bear away. This may not be sufficient to keep a straight course, particularly on the wind, so you may have to rig something at the bow to help keep her head off; a

165

storm jib set flying to the spinnaker pole topping lift and tacked on the weather rail-cap can either be sheeted to windward or leeward of the mast and will give a great deal of control over direction. Trial and error is the key here, remembering that sail area at the extreme ends of the boat will have the most effect and that you can sheet the sail so that it is aback if necessary. You can rig a storm jib on the backstay if sail area aft is needed for directional control.

Deck Fittings

A not infrequent occurrence of damage is to deck fittings. Draw the attention of the skipper or watch master to any crack you happen to see in a fitting, no matter how small it is. Action now could save the fitting from more serious damage later. This includes stranding of wires, starting of planks, bolts pulling or bending, or hairline cracks in castings and fibreglass. Most well-run boats keep a defects book.

Sails

A six inch tear or unsewn seam in a sail can go from one end to the other in seconds. Don't waste time discussing it; point it out to the skipper or watch leader who should order the sail down instantly, or the sailmaker will have a 30 foot rip to mend rather than the original six inches. Try to spot exactly where the hole is in relation to a fixed point in the sail, so that it can be more easily located later.

Leaks

If a wooden boat is holed it is usually possible to nail a board or boards over the inside of the hole, with sailcloth or some other padding as a sealer underneath the board; this will often suffice as a temporary leak stopper. A fibreglass boat presents a different problem and any form of underwater hole will have to be stuffed with canvas or bedding, which must be held down by props or stays. If there is a hole above water, or one which can be made to come above water by going onto a particular tack, which can thus be dried out properly, emergency fibreglass repair kits can do a useful job on a small hole and will be quite fast after about half an hour; suitable kits are sold in garages. In a full scale emergency try lashing a sail or piece of canvas right round the outside of the hull; the pressure of water trying to enter is supposed to force the sail into the hole and so help stop the gap (I'm glad to say that I have never

166

tried this). One of the Offshore Racing Council's emergency requirements is a supply of soft wood plugs; these can be driven into small holes where they will swell on contact with water and stop leaks.

Distress Signals

The internationally recognised distress signals are as follows (get to know them well in case you should see them on another boat at any time):

1 A gun or other explosive signal fired at intervals of about a minute.
2 A continuous sounding of any fog-signalling apparatus.
3 Rockets or shells, throwing red stars fired one at a time at short intervals.
4 A signal made by radiotelegraphy or by any other signalling method consisting of the group $\cdots - - - \cdots$ in Morse Code.
5 A signal sent by radiotelephony consisting of the spoken word 'Mayday'.
6 The International Code Signal of distress indicated by NC.
7 A signal consisting of a square flag having above or below it a ball or anything resembling a ball.
8 Flames on the vessel (as from a burning tar barrel, oil barrel, shirt soaked in oil held up on an oar or spinnaker pole or an oily rag in a bucket).
9 A rocket parachute flare or a hand flare showing a red light.
10 A smoke signal giving off a volume of orange-coloured smoke.
11 Slowly and repeatedly raising and lowering arms outstretched to each side.

In addition, the ensign flown upside down, while not officially recognised, is generally accepted as a distress signal.

Conserve pyrotechnics until you are fairly sure that they will be seen. If you loose off everything in a grand firework display at the sound of the first aircraft engine, you may find that he is in cloud and you are not spotted, so you need something for a searching ship later. You should normally wait until you can see an aircraft before firing a rocket and, even then, it is better if the machine is flying

167

towards you. An aircraft, of course, cannot hear a gun or fog signal and is unlikely to read code flags unless it comes down to have a close look.

Abandon Ship

When abandoning ship, if there is time try and take into the inflatable liferaft or dinghy with you warm clothes (if there is a wet suit aboard that's best of all), the distress flares, the first aid kit, some food and water, a torch, something to bail with and a knife. When safely in the dinghy, check on the crew, inspect for leaks, stream the drogue, clear water out of the bottom and rig the shelter. Huddle together for warmth, and exercise the arms and legs just enough to keep circulation going properly.

If you are in the water without a dinghy, it is agreed nowadays that exercise causes the blood to circulate more quickly, rise to the surface and shed heat from the body. Swimming is therefore not to be encouraged, even though it may give an illusion of warmth through increased circulation. Even short distances become too far for strong swimmers to cover in cold weather, for the water is viscous, the cold causes cramp and the body suffers from hypothermia. There is a medical reflex which causes gasping for breath and failure to control breathing when a person is suddenly plunged into cold seas which are splashing into his face; this is a further barrier to swimming. Keep still and control the breath so that you don't take in a lot of water.

Unless they are dragging you down, you should keep your clothes on because they afford warmth, even when immersed in water. Stay with the other survivors for moral support (if it looks like a long wait, tie yourselves together) and near any floating wreckage to make spotting easier for the rescue services.

11
What's Different About Offshore Racing?

Social

Whether you have raced before or not, you may have done some cruising either coastal or offshore; you may have done some racing round the cans. What then, is the difference in offshore racing?

In a word it is: tempo.

Racing offshore demands, as we have seen, more than 100 per cent effort for 25 hours a day. You are permanently on call, you have to drive yourself and the boat the whole time you are on deck, you cannot afford the luxury of a breather even to heave to in a gale, you have to keep going in the face of seasickness. Tactics between boats and exploitation of the rules play a smaller part offshore, and the effort has to be maintained out of sight of other boats and at night. If you let up, the others will be through you and down to the vino having signed their declarations, while you are still bucking the tide to get round that last headland.

Having said all this, I must relate my memories of the Dinard race as long ago as 1948. I was sailing in a 50 foot yawl called *Amokura* when she was owned by Ruth and Ernest Harston. We were close fetching towards the Casquets in a good breeze when Ruth announced lunch. And what a lunch. We had roast chicken followed by peaches in brandy. As I sat back on the settee afterwards I looked at the owner.

'We're not going to win this race, you know,' I said. 'But by Heaven I'm going to remember it.'

We didn't and I have.

The question asked above can also be put: what is different about cruising? First and foremost you are required to be sociable on a cruise. The object is to sit back and enjoy each other's company both ashore and afloat. I'm not saying that you can be surly and taciturn when racing, for there are moments of social enjoyment offshore which should be grasped and you do not want to be an irritating element to get everyone else's backs up. But when cruising there is more time for a yarn and relaxation, indeed you can become a nuisance if you are for ever dashing about trying to improve the set of the mainsail or suggesting a headsail change as soon as the wind alters by a couple of knots. You should exercise caution to prevent the keyed up racing feeling from creeping into a lazy cruise. If you don't, you'll have the rest of the crew fidgeting about altering sheets, suggesting the spinnaker, reckoning they can steer a better course and, before long, they will begin to snap at each other and you will all wonder why you are getting so excited.

The Opposition

But racing is another thing. A crew needs the spur of competition to stay on the top line and this is not always easy to achieve out of sight of land and all other yachts. It is at this time that you can give the right sort of impetus to the crew's efforts by a casual enquiry as to

XVII   *Dolce far Niente*   Lunch aboard *Gitana IV* in the middle of the most gruelling race in the British sailing calendar! Baron de Rothschild is in sunglasses and those bottles on the table came from his own vineyard. It's not all hell and high water.   *Author*

170

the skipper's estimate of the competitor you last saw just astern at dusk, or whether he thinks that you will get to a certain turning point before the tide turns. Don't harp on it, but start the ball rolling and then, when you have been discussing the chances of the opposition for a bit, you will all feel that little bit more inclined to change to a lighter headsail, or to fine-trim the spinnaker or genoa sheet easing it out, pulling it in, easing it out again in the never ending search for an extra yard or two of speed. You won't have another boat neck and neck with you to urge you on, but you will have a mental picture of one storming along with a crew of super-men all doing the right thing with effortless ease.

And this brings me to another point. Don't allow yourself to get downhearted at mistakes. The yacht which can finish a race and say quite honestly that she did not make a single mistake, or lose any time through faulty judgement or drill, is a very rare bird indeed. So, although you got your spinnaker wrapped round the forestay, or you now reckon that you tacked at the wrong moment, don't lose sight of the fact that your principal rival may have sailed into a flat patch, may have broken some gear or may, for all their alleged superiority in sail drill and the fact that they all wear identical red (or blue or green) uniforms, have failed to carry their spinnaker as early as you did (they didn't free off fifteen degrees or so in correct anticipation of a wind shift later). Stick to it and you may get a pleasant surprise.

Ship's Routine

It is normal when cruising to be somewhat short handed on board. If, therefore, you are aspiring to offshore racing, it must be supposed that you will be strong and healthy so, while you would find yourself the strongest link in the chain cruising, you will probably be the weakest when racing offshore, due principally to lack of experience. When cruising there will usually be women aboard who, while they can make as knowledgeable crew members as anyone else, are not always able to tail onto an anchor chain or hoist a spinnaker with quite the same beef as a man. Learn to respect their judgement and ability, however, for many of them know more about sailing than a lot of men. Even if a woman only thinks that she knows a lot, you have to give tactful ear to what she says if she is the owner's wife. This may not be as easy as it sounds, particularly if she suggests something which you know to be wrong (either nautically or morally). You have to keep the peace and there can be no more certain way of disturbing it than to tell the owner's wife that she doesn't know what she is talking about – unless it be to take her off to a French night club when the race is over in order to teach her a thing or two *à deux*.

You will often find when cruising that the owner has experience of other people's yachts which is limited to the type of meal which can be served and whether ice can be stored for more than a day. On the other hand you may have sailed in as many as a dozen different boats, with as many opportunities for picking up tips and hints on various aspects of sail drill and equipment. Now there may very well be a perfectly good reason why one boat uses individual sail ties to lash the mainsail to the boom when stowed and why another uses a simplifed system of shockcord and hooks; there may even be a perfectly bad reason for it, such as prejudice. You need to sound the ground carefully before suggesting a new idea: what may seem an improvement to you may hold untold memories of a snarl-up for the owner. But most owners are grateful for suggestions to ease the chores of crewing, if they are put tactfully. Either find a way of talking about the problem disinterestedly, or even introduce the idea by incorporating it as though you imagined it were already in use (or else keep quiet and don't try and be bossy if the moment is not ripe).

'The snap shackle seems to have come off the spinnaker staysail tack pendant. If you've got a spare, I'll put it back.'

'Don't throw that washing-up liquid bottle away; I'll wash it out and put cooker fuel in it so we can squirt it into the stove more easily.'

But less unobtrusive would be:

'If you've got a couple of old tennis balls, I'll shin up the mast and fit them on the crosstree ends as anti-chafe pads when we get into port.' (Owner immediately puts away his tennis racquet and hands over the balls.)

Customs

There is one aspect where cruising and racing have a common frontier. When you return from abroad be honest with the customs.

Whether it is because we share a love of the sea with the waterguard or because they are softhearted (!), Customs officers usually lean over backwards to be easy on yachtsmen. This is a special relationship which it would be foolish to put in jeopardy and it is the duty of every crewman to play fair. Apart from anything else, you will be a guest on somebody else's yacht, so don't give your host a bad name through your dishonesty.

Going Ashore

When going ashore in a strange port on an overnight stop between passage races, make sure that the boat is tidy before you leave. Stop all appropriate headsails and spinnakers ready for the next day, check off the fuel and seacocks and see that your bunk is spread out ready for occupation (if you come back late and others are already asleep, you won't be blessed as you struggle to make it up in the dark).

Leaving the Yacht

When it's all over and the crew is dispersing, make sure that you don't leave any unfinished jobs behind you. The boat was ready when you came aboard, see that she will be the same for the next race. The skipper should keep a defects list so that items of repair beyond local resources can be noted for action by the boatyard during the week. A final shutting-down checklist is a good idea, to include such items as seacocks, fuel, gas, water, stowage of gear, electrics, instruments, bo'sunry, engine, perishable food and the like; I have put one at Appendix D.

Navigation

Although blue water sailors would deny it strongly, navigation on a race offshore calls for greater accuracy than it does when cruising. The cruising man can afford to allow himself a mile or two in order to be certain of arriving up tide of a particular headland or turning point. If the racing man is a couple of miles out and the wind goes light, he has chucked away anything up to an hour (more if the wind drops altogether); if he arrives down tide and the wind is light, he may have chucked away six hours. The yachts which consistently win races make their landfalls right on the nose.

I agree that most offshore racers, in Classes I and II anyway, are equipped with more sophisticated electronics than their cruising sisters (although they are not always allowed by the rules to use all the aids available), largely because owners who race the heavy metal can usually afford the high cost involved. On the other hand the navigator's compartment is small and his equipment has to be used when all concerned are short of sleep, often when the boat is lying on her ear pitching and tossing with water flying across the chart table, yet still the demands of accuracy have to be met.

In a gale the average cruising boat will heave to, lie a-hull or run before it streaming warps. This used to be the drill for the offshore racing fleet until well into the nineteen forties, when modern design and construction proved seaworthy enough to be driven through the water on the correct course for the next mark. Almost overnight yachts like John Illingworth's legendary *Myth of Malham* brought a new dimension to racing, and they cleaned up in heavy weather because they kept going when the others had stopped.

Specialisation

The man who, besides an all-round ability as a crew, has some specialist skill as a bonus will more easily find a berth in a racing crew. Winchmen are not difficult to find, but someone who can coax an extra quarter of a knot out of a boat as well is much sought after.

Navigator

If, after all this, you have a hankering to become an offshore racing navigator, you will join a band of dedicated men who are on a hiding to nothing. If the race is won, the skipper, helmsman and crew get the credit; if it is lost, the blame is not infrequently heaped on the luckless navigator. But there is a certain satisfaction to be derived from raising a light or landfall exactly where and when you predict, after the Consol has gone on the blink and the night watch has produced as large a cocked hat D/F fix as you have ever seen.

'Sorry nav. It was dawn and I think the bearings must have been a bit distorted.'

Foredeck

An owner will cherish a good foredeck master as he would an obliging bank manager. If you can govern the spinnaker in all its moods and learn to gybe it from one reach to the other, controlling the foredeck gang as a symphony orchestra is controlled by its conductor so that everything is smooth and co-ordinated, you will be able to command a place in any crew. To so this you must not only know everybody's job backwards, you must be able to do it better than anybody else, yet you must be able to get them to do it as well as you can. You need eyes in the back of your head, you must have the gift of second sight so that you know what other boats are going to do at close quarters, you must be a mind reader so that you know your own helmsman's intentions before he does himself. You will be the iron man of the boiler house, a bastard to the crew when they make mistakes and you will be adored by that same crew for your discipline and uncompromising refusal to accept second best. It takes years of solid apprenticeship and there is no substitute for experience.

Cook

On some boats everybody takes his turn at cooking, possibly standing out of a watch when he is on culinary duties. This means that each crew member has a full night's sleep once in however many days there are crew members; five or six being a good average and also the length of an equally average Fastnet or Bermuda race for that sized boat. But every crew likes to have a full time cook, who can also be expected to turn his hand to a bit of simple sheet pulling if absolutely necessary. So, if you are not tough enough, young enough, quick enough or clever enough to stand up to the pace of the upper deck, yet you still want to be welcomed aboard an offshore racer, try cooking (but choose a big boat which can afford to have a specialist man aboard). You must be able to produce appetising meals from an endless series of tins prepared on a tiny swaying hotplate with big wet men pushing you out of the way, cursing you, shouting for coffee, groaning that they don't feel like your *pièce de résistance* (over an hour to prepare) or knocking the stew into the bilges as it comes up to the boil. In your own way you too

175

will be a dedicated man – and you will need an iron stomach into the bargain.

Sail Trimmer

A sail trimmer does not have a full time job, but one who knows his onions is worth his weight in gold to a top class offshore racing yacht. He must know the boat concerned well: the hull characteristics; the limitations of each sail; the calibre of the crew; and the quality of each helmsman. Above all he must know what he is trying to achieve. He it is who can say with certainty when the boat will carry a spinnaker to advantage on a shy reach or whether she will go better under a double head rig and, having said his piece, he can organise things so that the sails pull to best advantage. A good sail trimmer can usually expect to get another quarter of a knot out of a boat when he comes on watch in the early stages of shaking down a strange crew; later, he should have passed on enough of his lore to ensure that the other watch can get the same results. It takes time in the same boat, constant practice and a thorough knowledge of the theory of sails. It also needs a systematic approach, for he should keep a chart of sails, sea and wind conditions, sheeting details and the resulting boat speeds. Only then will he be able to get the right sails in their basic trim to give best results and then adjust the controls until he gets the speed he knows he should obtain. He cannot, however, expect to sit idly by once all this has been done; no crew can afford to carry a man whose only job gives him five minutes work in every hour, no matter how vital those five minutes may be. He has to be a regular crewman, doing a normal crew's job for most of the time, but his expert knowledge will assure him a regular place in the crew even if he isn't quite so quick or strong as the next man.

Technical

A man who can add knowledge of engines or electronics to his usefulness as a crewman will have a better chance of an invitation to come a second time than one who relies solely on pulling the right sheet at the right time. The skill is by no means essential to the race, but may be a welcome bonus in time of need. The same can be said of someone who can wield a needle and palm to repair a torn sail.

176

Helmsman

Finally we come to the job of helmsman. Everybody has to take a turn at the wheel or tiller in an offshore race but, if you can be relied upon to get the boat to windward better than the next man, steer under a spinnaker on a wild day or even get the start you want every time, you will have reached the position everybody would like to attain but few can either afford or aspire to. Let's face it, it is asking quite a lot for a man to go and spend rather more than a year's salary on a yacht only to hand her over for somebody else to steer most of the time; you've got to be good to merit the reward. If you are that good, always try to remember to hand the helm back to the owner for the last mile or so to the finish. It is fitting that the owner should take his boat over the line at the end of a long and hard race, and it is therefore courteous to remember it. If conditions are tricky and he thinks that you will make a better job of it, or that the boat might lose vital seconds during the handover, he will soon tell you to carry on.

General Crewman

We started this book with the intention of learning a bit more about being a good crew member, and it is fitting at the end that we should come down to earth from the rarified atmosphere surrounding navigation and helmsmanship. If you learn to be a good all-rounder you will always command a berth. Know your stuff, don't be afraid of hard or dity work, co-operate and don't try to hide ignorance; keep it going cheerfully until the end. When it's all over, help clear things up and do any repairs before you catch your train home.

'Nice to have had you aboard, and thanks for helping out at the end. I'd never have got that loo cleared by myself. What are you doing for the second week in August?'

Appendix A

Anti-Seasickness Drugs

Approved name	Trade or proprietary name	Tablet size	Adult dose	Time to take effect	Frequency
Cyclizine	Marzine Valoid	50 mg	50–100 mg	4–6 hours	3 times a day
Dimenhydrinate	Dramamine Gravol	50 mg	50–100 mg	2–4 hours	3 times a day
Promethazine hydrochloride	Phenergan	10 mg and 25 mg	25 mg	6–8 hours or night before	2 or 3 times a day
Promethazine theoclate	Avomine	25 mg	25 mg	6–8 hours or night before	2 or 3 times a day
Scopolamine (hyoscine)	Kwells Joy-rides	0·3 mg 0·15 mg	0·3– 0·6 mg	1 hour	2–3 hourly
Cinnarizine	Stugeron	0·15 mg	15 mg	Start previous day	3 times a day

Based on a table published in *Yachting World*, by kind permission of the Editor

Notes

1 Every individual varies in the way that he reacts to almost any drug, particularly antihistamines.

2 If a person is taking other drugs quite legitimately from his doctor, beware lest whatever he takes for seasickness has some difficult reaction with the drug he is having. In such cases, consult the doctor in question.

3 The dose for children can be calculated by working on a weight-for-dose basis: a 75 lb child will need half the dose of a 150 lb adult. If in doubt, ask your doctor.

Appendix B

Typical Joining Instructions

Yacht　...　　...　　...　　...　　...　　...　　...　　...　　...

Race　...　　...　　...　　...　　...　　...　　...　　...　　...

Boat's mooring　...　　...　　...　　...　　...　　...　　...　　...

Start time　...　　... o'clock on (*date*)　...　　...　　...　　...

Joining time　...　　... o'clock on (*date*)　...　　...　　...　　...

Leave moorings　...　　... o'clock on (*date*)　...　　...　　...　　...

Personal gear. No suitcases; use soft dunnage bag. Shoregoing gear plus one/two/three changes of sailing clothes. Deck shoes or ankle length sea-boots only on board. Passports. Foul weather clothing. Car parking.

Ship's supply. Sleeping bags. Lifejackets, Harnesses. Food and drink.

Duties/Watches. Skipper. Navigator. Foredeck master. Cook. Port watch. Starboard watch. Watch-keeping times. Drill for handing over watch (punctuality; watch going below to call reliefs with hot drink and biscuits).

Extracts from Ship's Standing Orders

Wearing of harnesses and lifejackets.
Man overboard drill.
Calling the skipper/navigator on deck.
Meal times.
Cleaning ship.
Alcohol.
Customs officers.

Finance Crewing fee. Contribution to sustenance.

Expected time of finishing. Time. Port of finish.

Return passage.

Appendix C

Pre-race Check Lists

Before Moving Out

1	Sea cocks	On
2	Engine	Fuel, water and electrics on
3	Navigation	Charts and books; racing instructions; weather forecast
4	Instruments and radio	On and checked; impellers; batteries; compasses; time signal from radio
5	Flags	Class flag and ensign
6	Galley	Food and water aboard; cooking fuel on or filled
7	Personal gear	Aboard and stowed
8	Emergency equipment	Checked and stowed; liferaft; flares; lifebuoys; dan buoy; harnesses; lifejackets; first aid; fire extinguishers; emergency water; soft wood plugs; bilge pumps

Under Way

1	Warps and fenders	Stowed
2	Instruments	Functioning
3	Sails	Sorted and stopped
4	Ship's gear	Sheets and guys rove; winch handles; reefing gear; torches
5	Watches and duties	Allocated
6	Personal gear	Stowed for sea
7	Food	Stowed

Before the Start

1	Seacocks	On or off as required
2	Engine	Fuel and water off; propeller set for racing (leave diesel fuel on)
3	Racing instructions	Checked for start time and line
4	Galley	Stowed for sea
5	Ensign	Stowed

Appendix D

Post-race Check List

Leaving the Boat

1	Seacocks	Off
2	Engine	Fuel, water and electrics off (diesel on)
3	Navigation	Charts stowed
4	Instruments and radio	Off. Impellers withdrawn
5	Flags	Stowed or flying as required
6	Galley	Fuel off; dishes cleaned and stowed; perishables ashore, rest stowed
7	Sails	Battens out of mainsail; sails dried, stopped and stowed; torn sails ashore for repair
8	Repairs	Complete or in hand
9	Personal gear	Packed and cleared; bunks made up as required
10	Ship's gear	Stowed. Lifebuoys, liferaft, winch handles, sheets, guys, compasses
11	Halyards	Secure and frapped
12	Moorings	Secure. Check aloft for clash of spreaders with neighbour; fenders
13	Anti-chafe	Warps parcelled where necessary
14	Helm	Lashed or locked
15	Lights	As required (anchor light)
16	Defects list	Make up and give to yard or person who will make them good

Appendix E

The Beaufort Wind Scale

Beaufort Force	Wind speed at 33 ft (10 m) height			Description
	knots	mph	m/sec	
0	0– 1	0– 1	0·0– 0·2	Calm
1	1– 3	1– 3	0·3– 1·5	Light
2	4– 6	4– 7	1·6– 3·3	Light
3	7–10	8–12	3·4– 5·4	Gentle
4	11–16	13–18	5·5– 7·9	Moderate
5	17–21	19–24	8·0–10·7	Fresh
6	22–27	25–31	10·8–13·8	Strong
7	28–33	32–38	13·9–17·1	Near gale
8	34–40	39–46	17·2–20·7	Gale
9	41–47	47–54	20·8–24·4	Strong gale
10	48–55	55–63	24·5–28·4	Whole gale
11	56–63	64–72	28·5–32·6	Whole gale
12	64–71	73–82	32·7–36·9	Hurricane

Appendix F

Glossary of Terms

This is not intended to be complete, but to help a dinghy sailor unfamiliar with bigger boats.

Admiralty type anchor	Another name for a Fisherman anchor
Alcohol fuel	Spirit or methylated spirit cooking fuel
Back (a sail)	To sheet a sail to windward so that it pushes rather than pulls
Back (wind)	The wind backs when it shifts in an anti-clockwise direction
Bee blocks	Fairleads for reef pendants at the outer end of a boom, provided by battens of wood with holes in them, fastened to the side of the boom
Bellmouth end	The open end of a spinnaker pole, with a wire or wires emerging from it which fasten to the guy and can be drawn onto the end of the pole
Bend (a sail)	To rig or fasten a sail to a boat, usually to a spar or spars
Bight	A loop in a rope
Breast rope	A mooring rope from the bow or stern of a boat, running directly ashore abeam
Bunt (of a sail)	The main area of the sail
Bustle	A slight swelling in the underwater lines of a hull between the after edge of the keel and the forward side of the skeg
Canvas	Any sailcloth, either synthetic or natural fibre
Catenary action	The elastic effect given to an anchor chain by the rise and fall of the length of chain as it hangs in a curve from the boat to the anchor on the seabed

Check (a sheet)	Ease it out
CQR anchor	A double ploughshare anchor without stock
Dan buoy	A small buoy with a flag on a pole which is weighted at its lower end so that it floats upright at all times. When thrown overboard the flag, which is some eight feet above sea level, will mark a man in the water alongside from some distance
Danforth anchor	A parallel fluked anchor without stock.
Dog watch	Two short watches in the naval watch system, from 1600–1800 hours and from 1800–2000 hours. They prevent a recurrence of the same duties for the same watch personnel
Downhaul	Any system of tackle arranged to haul down a spar or sail
Drogue	A small sea anchor incorporated into a rubber liferaft or a lifebuoy to prevent it drifting with the wind
Fall	The free part of a halyard, to which the pull is applied
Fin and skeg	Hull configuration with a small fin keel and a separate skeg onto which the rudder is hung
Fisherman anchor	The traditional type of anchor with stock, shank and two flukes
Flashing (light)	A light is flashing when the darkened periods are longer than the light periods
Frap	To wrap or restrain halyards (and other lines up the mast) in order to stop them rattling in the wind when moored at night
Genniker	A sail which rates and is set under the spinnaker rules, but which is cut flat enough to set with the apparent wind about 45 degrees forward of the beam
Hand (a sail)	Lower and remove a sail
Handed	Propellers and winches are said to be handed when they rotate in opposite directions
Handicap	A yacht's handicap is spoken of as her IOR rating. This can be expressed as her TCF (time correction factor), which is a factor by which her elapsed time is multiplied to reach her corrected time; or her BSF (basic speed factor), which shows the average

185

number of seconds she is reckoned to take to cover one sea mile. TCF is a time-on-time, and BSF is a time-on-distance method of handicap. The IOR rating can also be expressed more broadly as a hypothetical length in feet. A second and less technical handicap system for yachts of a particular type or class, is the Portsmouth yardstick system. This is based on known performance and results and, while it applied principally to dinghies, smaller series production yachts also have a PY number. A particular handicap is expressed as a number, which usually ranges 20 either side of 100; the lower the number the faster the boat

Harden sheets	Haul in the sheets
Head rope	A mooring rope from the bow, which stretches forward from the boat to the quayside
Impeller	A small propeller, usually on a retractable probe, which sticks out underneath the hull to measure water speed
Lazy sheet or guy	Where a spinnaker has a sheet and a guy on each clew, the one not in use is termed the lazy one
Mouse	To close the open end of a hook with a seizing, or to secure the two parts of sister hooks with twine
Muzzle	To smother a sail as it comes down, in order to prevent it being blown about
Occulting (light)	A light is occulting when the light periods are longer than the dark periods
Parcel	To wrap a rope with canvas as an anti-chafe measure
Parrel (beads)	A line threaded with wooden balls so that it may be fastened round a spar and move easily along it
Pay out	Ease out
Preventer	A rope or wire rigged as a guy to prevent a spar from uncontrolled swing
Powerpoint	The position of maximum camber in a sail
Rail cap	The top of the toerail at the edge of the deck
Reef cleats	Fairleads at the end of the boom for passage of reef pendants
Riding turn	One turn of a rope on a winch which has ridden up over its neighbour

Rode	Any warp, chain or wire used for anchoring
Skeg	The small fin, separate from the keel, on which the rudder is hung
Slack up	Ease out
Slat sail	A tall thin sail set in front of the mainsail when the boat is off the wind, in order to clean up the airflow to leeward
Spanker	See Genniker
Standing part	The part of a halyard or sheet under tension, which is not hauled on
Springs	Mooring lines which are taken from aft in the boat forward to the quay and from forward aft to the quay, arranged so that the boat does not move fore and aft
Start (a sheet)	Ease out
Stern gland	The watertight gland in the stern tube, through which the propeller shaft passes; it is kept watertight by means of a greaser
Tallboy	See Slat sail
Toe-rail	The raised part of the outside edge of the deck
Transit or Range	When two objects or lights are in line
Trim tab	A small tab on the aft edge of the keel, which can be adjusted while sailing
Tripping line	A rope secured to the crown of an anchor so that, if it hooks into an obstruction and will not break out, the anchor can be pulled forward to clear it
Two blocks	When the blocks of a purchase are as close together as they will go, the purchase is said to be two-blocks or chock-a-block
Vang	A strop or rope used to hold down a spar, usually the main boom
Veer (chain)	Pay out chain
Veer (wind)	The wind veers when it shifts in a clockwise direction
Wear ship	The original meaning was the same as gybe; it is more often nowadays taken to mean the exact opposite, particularly when a boat is tacked as a safety measure where a gybe might be dangerous. To avoid ambiguity the word is best not used

Appendix G

Ten Commandments of Offshore Racing

1 Give nothing away at any time; maintain 120 per cent effort.

2 Know everyone else's job and be ready to get your hands dirty.

3 Be clear-headed.

4 Be safe sensibly.

5 Cooperate and avoid irritation.

6 Concentrate and allow to concentrate.

7 Be tidy and quiet.

8 Don't bluff.

9 Maintain morale.

10 Keep it up to the end.

Bibliography

Admiralty Manual of Seamanship   *Volume I* 1964
At Home in Deep Waters   *Bruce Fraser*   1965
Cornelius Shields on Sailing   *Cornelius Shields*   1964
Crewing Offshore   *Alan Hollingsworth*   1964
Further Offshore   *John Illingworth*   1972
Heavy Weather Sailing   *K. Adlard Coles*   1972
Learning to Race   *H. A. Calahan*   1947
Ocean Racing and Offshore Yachts   *Peter Johnson*   1970
Race Your Boat Right   *Arthur Knapp Jnr.*   1963
Sailing Boats   *Uffa Fox*   1960
Sailing Theory and Practice   *C. A. Marchaj*   1973
Sailing to Win   *Robert N. Bavier*   1948
Sails   *Jeremy Howard-Williams*   1973
Yacht Racing; the Aerodynamics of Sails   *Manfred Curry*   1948